Haynes
Wooden
Toy Manual

Published in September 2012

A catalogue record for this book is available
from the British Library

ISBN 978 0 85733 220 2

Library of Congress catalog control no. 2012936195

Haynes Publishing,
Sparkford, Yeovil, Somerset BA22 7JJ, UK
Tel: +44 (0) 1963 442030
Fax: +44 (0) 1963 440001
E-mail: sales@haynes.co.uk
Website: www.haynes.co.uk

Haynes North America, Inc.,
861 Lawrence Drive, Newbury Park,
California 91320, USA

Printed in the USA by Odcombe Press LP,
1299 Bridgestone Parkway, La Vergne, TN 37086

Workshop photography: Robert Coleman
Studio photography: James Mann
Design: Richard Parsons

A message from Paul Gemmell, Business Development Manager for Dremel

Being a child of the '70s, I have some hazy memories of TV back in
those days. Strikingly, one of these memories is of a BBC afternoon
magazine show *Pebble Mill*. Maybe it was the boxed construction
of the studios, or just the fact that we only had three channels and
it was on five days a week that makes it so vivid in my mind.

Anyway, when you're growing up you never know whose path
you'll cross as you make your way in life. I never thought that all these
years later I'd be working closely with one of the stars of the *Pebble
Mill* show which had strangely stuck in my mind – Richard Blizzard.

Richard is multi-faceted: a TV presenter, author, musician,
craftsman, engineer, husband and father. Add to this the fact that
Richard is a wonderfully articulate man who is passionate about
everything that he does, and you have all the qualities that, I believe,
made him such a television natural.

As a hobbyist with a serious devotion to model railways and
woodworking, Richard is the author of 28 books that, although
the subject matter varies, have a common theme of engaging
with readers and inspiring them – regardless of ability – to have
a go and make something.

In the time that I've known Richard, both as a business contact
and now – hopefully not presumptuously on my part – as a friend, he
has provided no end of inspiration and applications for our products,
often finding new uses for existing products and offering insight on
applications for new ones.

The Haynes *Wooden Toy Manual* you've purchased has been
produced with a level of dedication and vigour that you'd think had
come from a man with a few less miles on the clock, but this is the
energy and life that Richard brings to his projects and books. It will
enable you to complete simple wooden projects to delight children
and grandchildren, such as the mouse and cheese block, and larger,
more complex projects such as the wheelbarrow and the crane, that
will test you and help you develop your woodworking skills in easy-to-
follow, understandable stages.

Even today the books Richard wrote in the '70s remain some of
the 'most borrowed' from UK libraries, and I have no doubt that this
marvellous manual will also gain a place in UK hobbyists' hearts,
allowing Richard's expertise and knowledge to continue inspiring
people for many generations to come.

Contents

Wooden Toy Manual

Introduction		6
Tools to do the job		8

1	Hammer & Pegs	12
2	Mouse & Cheese	20
3	Pull-along Train	26
4	Woodpecker Tree	40
5	Roundabout	48
6	Go-kart	58
7	Wheelbarrow	68
8	Market Stall	76
9	Tugboat	86
10	Playhouse	94
11	Rocking Elephant	102
12	Trike & Trailer	112
13	Pull-along Trolley	122
14	Pirate Ship	134
15	Farmyard	144
16	Ark & Animals	154
17	Crane	164
18	Articulated Lorry	174
19	Bagatelle	184
20	Labyrinth	192

Introduction

By Richard Blizzard

Wood is such a versatile material, and toys for children have been fashioned from it for thousands of years. Children have wonderful imaginations, so given even the most rudimentary of toys and their imaginations will take them far. The simple train and carriages become an express train, and a simple boat a galleon ready to fight off pirates as they sail the Spanish Main.

Toys are also wonderful for teaching children how things work – the crane truck with its adjustable boom, jack, ratchet winding handles and rotating body; the mouse that can only be threaded through certain holes in the 'cheese block'; and the hammer and pegs toy to make a good noise!

Toys made from wood are sturdy. They take wear and tear well and, if a breakage should occur, can be mended. Wooden toys can be passed from one generation to the next – re-varnished and polished they come up like new.

It should never be forgotten that a toy made with loving hands by a mother, father or grandfather will always be

something special. I've therefore tried to include a project for everyone, and if some of them look a little daunting then make something simple before trying your hand at a bigger project. The rocking elephant is great fun, but learn to use a jigsaw before you commit to this jumbo toy.

It's my hope that you'll use these basic designs simply as a starting point, and will embellish them with your own ideas and skills.

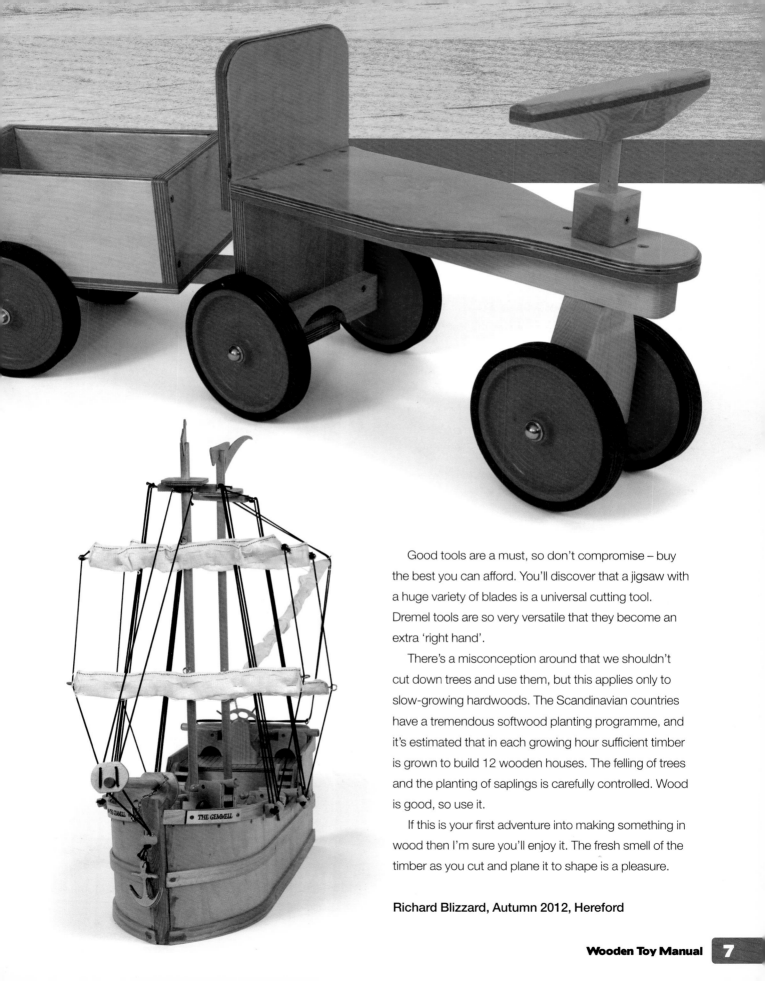

Good tools are a must, so don't compromise – buy the best you can afford. You'll discover that a jigsaw with a huge variety of blades is a universal cutting tool. Dremel tools are so very versatile that they become an extra 'right hand'.

There's a misconception around that we shouldn't cut down trees and use them, but this applies only to slow-growing hardwoods. The Scandinavian countries have a tremendous softwood planting programme, and it's estimated that in each growing hour sufficient timber is grown to build 12 wooden houses. The felling of trees and the planting of saplings is carefully controlled. Wood is good, so use it.

If this is your first adventure into making something in wood then I'm sure you'll enjoy it. The fresh smell of the timber as you cut and plane it to shape is a pleasure.

Richard Blizzard, Autumn 2012, Hereford

Tools to do the job

Technology has changed all of our lives and the way we do things. Tools haven't escaped this process, and although they might not look hugely different there are some very real changes. Tenon and hand saws were always resharpened with a file, but no longer – the majority now have case-hardened teeth which stay sharper much, much longer and, yes, are disposed of once they get blunt. Not just hand tools have changed – the battery screwdriver now has a lithium battery which holds its charge even in the cold, can be recharged at coffee time without damaging its memory, has a three-digit light system to tell you when to recharge, a light that shines exactly on the point where the drill/ screwdriver bit will meet the screw, a clutch, and a memory system when driving screws – wonderful!

Looking through the pictures in this book, don't be daunted because you haven't got all the latest tools. Most of the toys can be made with a basic toolkit. The electric tools just make things quicker and in some cases safer, and make it easier to carry out the job.

However, one absolute essential with either hand or power tools is that you do observe some basic safety rules:

1 Never work when you're tired.

2 Concentrate on the job – never answer the mobile when you're using tools.

3 Keep chisels, drill bits and all cutting-edge tools sharp – they really are so much safer that way. If you force a blunt chisel that's been used to open a paint can, you'll slip and most likely injure your hands. Chisel-sharpening stones,

and a jig to hold the chisel while sharpening it, are available at a small cost and will prove their worth over the years.

4 A hand saw that has propped open the greenhouse door for years is a dead loss – buy a new one. Tools that are designed to cut must be sharp, otherwise force is applied and it's then that accidents happen.

Eyes and ears

If you use a pillar drill you may well be advised to wear protective glasses. The Dremel grinders and shapers can also throw out some fine bits, so protect your eyes. The majority of electric saws, routers and sanders are noisy, but ear protectors are cheap and easily available, so use them.

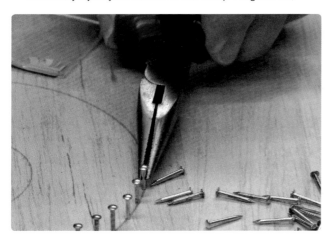

Tools

Top on my list of cutting tools is the jigsaw. It might originally have been conceived as a tool to cut jigsaws, but now, like all the tools, it has 'come of age', and can cut almost any material you like to try, provided that you have the correct blade. Blades are now easily interchangeable, and when rough cutting is required a pendulum action can be switched on which gives the jigsaw the ability to cut some really thick timber, boards etc. Fine blades are available to cut plywood without making ugly splinters on the surface. When cutting accurate shapes, a blower removes all the dust and allows you to follow your pencil line. Dust extraction is also designed into the body of the machine, so that you can clean up as you go. The speed at which the blade cuts is totally controllable by the trigger, enabling you to have full control.

Clamps and vices

It's important to hold things firmly when you're working. I've discovered by using the Dremel Project Table just how useful it is. This table has a good clamping system and you can work all around it. Timber can be clamped in place and the jigsaw can cut all around without the constant need to reposition it.

Ratchet clamps are so useful, in fact, you can never really have enough of them. They're extremely useful when you want to hold two pieces of timber together while the glue dries.

Cutting, sanding and routing

A newcomer to the woodworking world is the Dremel Trio. As its name suggests, this can perform three cutting operations. Its unique feature is a spiral cutter resembling a drill bit, but that's where the likeness stops. The circular cutter is a unique shape and will cut and shape timber with ease. The handle has a three-stage adjustment and enables the operator to see exactly the job they're doing. Simply push the cutter forward, and the powerful machine slices through timber – and, yes, without the spiral cutter snapping off. Fit it with a router cutter and it performs well. Fit a sanding band and you have a perfect method of smoothing off rough edges.

Sanding

When you make wooden toys it's essential to remove and round-off any corners or sharp edges. Bosch has a battery-powered sander that uses their new 18V lithium battery pack, and has a micro filter to catch all the dust. Dremel also make a band sanding drum, the Sander Band, that fits into their multitool and is very effective at rounding off corners and edges. It's also wonderful at enlarging holes to fit tight bolts or dowel rods – in fact it's one of the most efficient tools I've found for this task.

Boring holes

Drilling a hole as a pilot for a screw is simple, but other, larger holes requiring a little more skill are also needed for the toys in this book. The problem arises when you have to drill several holes in a piece of timber all at exactly 90° in both planes. Enter the drill stand!

For small holes there's the Dremel workstation, which will do excellent, accurate work.

For larger holes Bosch make a drill stand that will take a corded electric drill. This is quite a step up, and enables large, accurate holes to be bored with ease. The latest is a Bosch Pillar Drill that has such great features as a speed indicator and a cross-hairs laser light that will align exactly on the spot you've marked for the hole you need to drill. Perhaps one of its most excellent features is the clamping device that holds the timber very securely to the table and prevents any accidents. This clamp is a really valuable advance in bench drills and a real step forward in accident prevention.

Large, accurate sawing jobs

The playhouse is the largest project in this book – in reality it's like building a small shed. For this project it's vital that you cut the frames accurately at 90° in both planes. The frames are cut from timber 50mm square and it's important that the timbers butt together square at all the junctions. Compound mitre saws are designed to cut timber very accurately, not just at 90° but at practically any angle, including compound mitres. When the playhouse frames are covered with shiplap board this machine's ability to cross-cut accurately is invaluable. The larger machines have a sliding set of rails that make the width they're able to cross-cut to an advantage.

Safety features are good, with clamps to hold timber securely while being cut and a laser light to show exactly where the blade will cut the timber. These machines are available to hire from tool shops. Fast precise sawing of large timbers with these machines is excellent.

Shaping, cutting, moulding, sanding, routing, and useful accessories

Now, you'll soon discover that in all wooden toys and model making there's a great deal of fine woodworking required. Dremel manufacture a range of tools that make woodworking – particularly models and wooden toys – a pleasure. The basic Dremel power tool is digital, speeds being totally adjustable. This power unit fits into a variety of other accessories, plunge router accessory, shaper router table, a multipurpose cutting kit, a workstation that makes a very useful drill stand and a mini-saw attachment. In addition to these a vast number of cutters, reamers and polishing heads are available. I found the drum band-sanders absolutely great in so many shaping operations.

There's a glue gun in the range, and I found the instant hot glue ideal for securing small parts – only you have to work very quickly before the glue loses its heat.

Many of the cutting wheels and polishing wheels use Dremel's 'SpeedClic' system when changing heads. The range of ratchet clamps is excellent, and when gluing small parts together you can never have too many.

One of the most useful devices is the Project Table – I use it all the time. This is a small table whose top works as a screw vice. There are plastic moulded lugs that fit into the tabletop,

making it possible to clamp large objects. The Project Table is a really good table/vice workstation, which, if you don't have a workbench, with a piece of plywood underneath can be mounted on the kitchen table (necessary permission having been granted!).

Another of the 'separate' tools produced by Dremel is a soldering iron – a very upmarket one, the tip being heated by a ceramic burner. There's a range of tips to fit this device, and I used it for burning 'brick' on to the surface of buildings (see the farmhouse project). An engraving tool is also available, which works very effectively.

The latest tool from Dremel – and certainly one of the most useful to the toy maker – is the Moto-Saw. This is really a saw equipped to cut shapes in both plywood and soft/hard woods. The blade is very fine and will give an almost 'finished' cut to the wood. A large, deep frame enables it to cut lengthy pieces of timber. The Noah's Ark toy is a prime example of the usefulness of a saw like this. The saw can be clamped to a small table, which gives the operator full control of the cutting operation as the wood is offered to the blade.

Hammer & Pegs

Some may think that young children make sufficient noise without giving them a toy that will make even *more* noise. However, there's something therapeutic about thumping the wooden pegs with a wooden mallet until they're all through, and then turning the block over and thumping them back again!

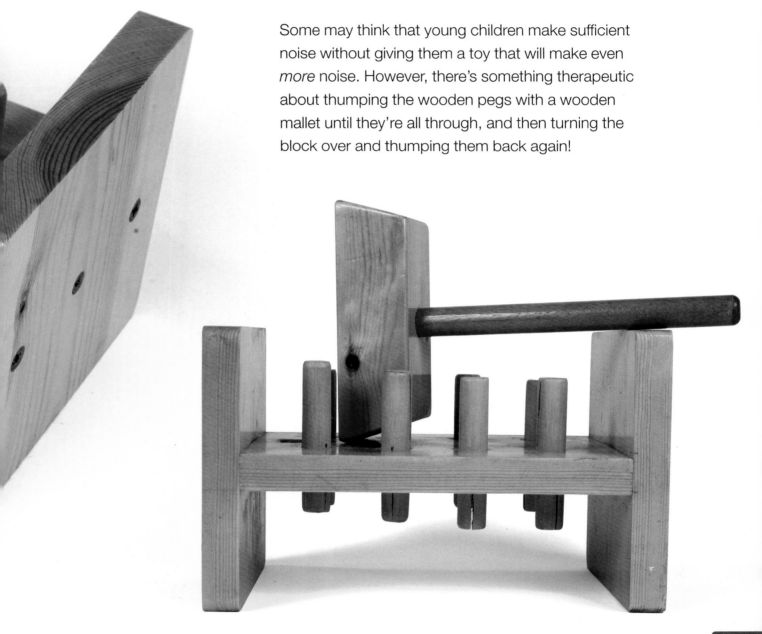

Hammer & Pegs

Project components

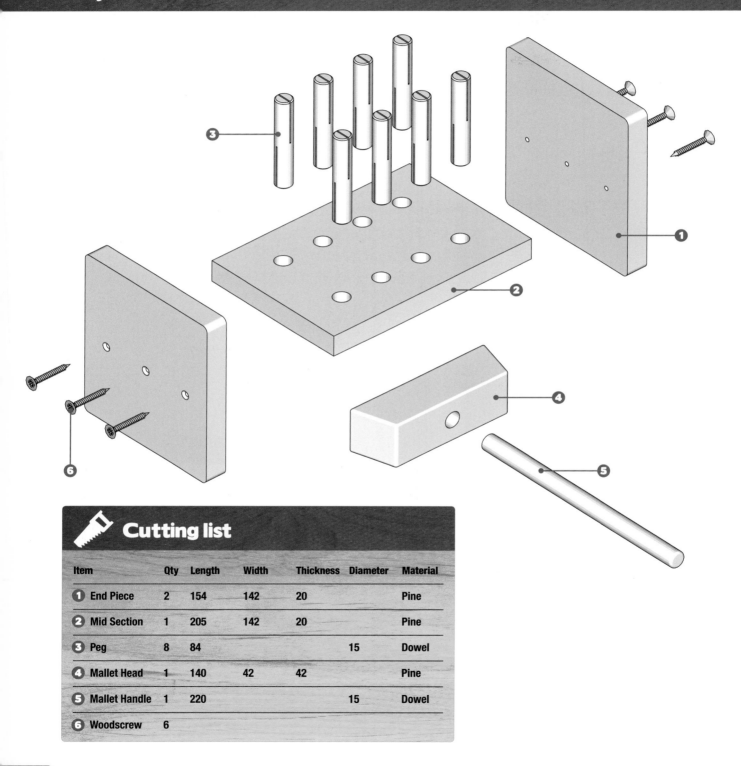

Cutting list

Item	Qty	Length	Width	Thickness	Diameter	Material
❶ End Piece	2	154	142	20		Pine
❷ Mid Section	1	205	142	20		Pine
❸ Peg	8	84			15	Dowel
❹ Mallet Head	1	140	42	42		Pine
❺ Mallet Handle	1	220			15	Dowel
❻ Woodscrew	6					

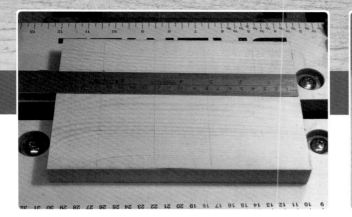

1 The timber is a piece of knot-free Nordic red pine. Avoid knots if possible – they weaken the structure.

2 Marking out the centres for the pegs. Do mark the peg centres clearly because when you start drilling there will be dust and chippings everywhere.

3 The peg board ready for holes to be drilled.

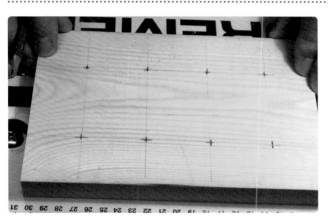

4 The Bosch bench drill has a clamp that holds the work firmly in place (swivelled sideways here, for the hole drilling to be seen). It also has a laser light with cross hairs so that you can hit the spot exactly.

5 Marking out the sides – there are three screw-holes to be drilled and countersunk.

6 Do mark in pencil lines, as this helps locate the peg board when you're assembling the parts.

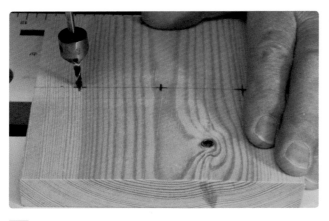

7 A drill with countersink attached is used. This is a very useful device as it drills and countersinks in one operation.

8 With the peg board clamped firmly in the vice, glue is applied to the end.

9 Position the end carefully before driving in the screws. The pencil lines were marked in earlier (see step 6).

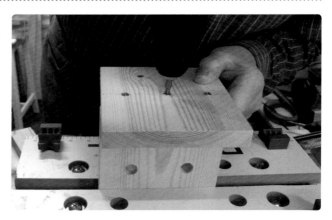

10 As you drive the screw in the glue has a tendency to make the parts slip, so check the pencil lines again.

11 Glue is now applied to the other end and screws are once again driven in.

12 Be certain that the screw seats itself in the countersunk hole, otherwise little fingers will get scratched.

13 The final screw is driven in, completing the construction of the peg board base.

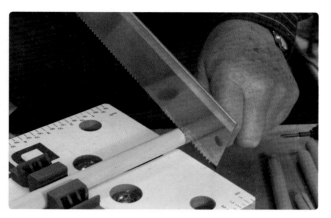

14 Dowel rods are held firmly in place allowing the pegs to be cut to length.

15 I used a Dremel Moto-Saw to cut halfway along the peg. The peg is then cut halfway along from the other end (turn the peg first to prevent it being cut in half). The peg needs to be a tight fit in the hole. The slots provide a friction fit.

16 A peg mounted in the block. If the peg is too tight then a Dremel tool is used with a circular sanding drum to open up the hole – do this carefully, otherwise the peg will drop through the hole.

17 A small mallet is marked up. An angle is marked on the end to provide a good striking surface.

18 Using a saw to cut the angle.

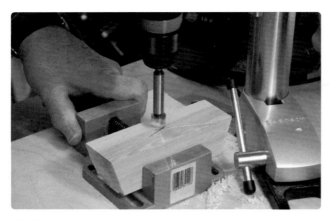

19 Mark the centre hole to take the handle. With the mallet head clamped in a portable vice (to show it more clearly), the hole for the handle is drilled through to the other side of the mallet head.

20 A slot is cut in the mallet handle with the Moto-Saw. The purpose of the slot is so that a wooden wedge can be driven in to prevent the head coming off.

21 Glue is applied to the handle and the handle is driven into the head.

22 The handle is secured to the head using a small wooden wedge, which is glued into the prepared slot.

23 The wedge is driven into the handle, and the surplus wedge end is cut off.

24 A battery-powered hand sander is used to round off all the corners.

25 Use the sander to work over the peg block, rounding off the edges.

26 Now check the pegs in the block – they should be tight.

27 Use the mallet to drive the pegs in. If the pegs are too tight, use a Dremel drum sander to enlarge the holes.

28 Finished peg block toy. I drilled an extra hole to take the mallet handle – well, it keeps things tidy!

Mouse & Cheese

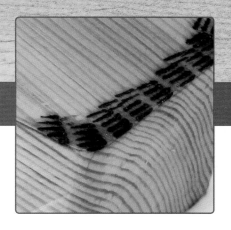

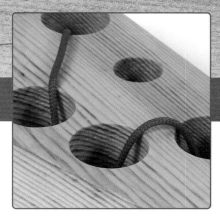

This is an old version of the 'shape sorter' toys that you can buy. Squares, triangles and oblong blocks are 'posted' into the correct holes and a child soon learns the differences. This version features a mouse that goes into different holes in a wooden 'cheese' block. The mouse, having eaten too well, cannot get into some holes. The game is simply to thread the mouse into the holes he can get in. You can make this as simple or as complicated as you wish just by changing hole sizes. You can even have a skinny mouse that's allowed in small holes.

Mouse & Cheese

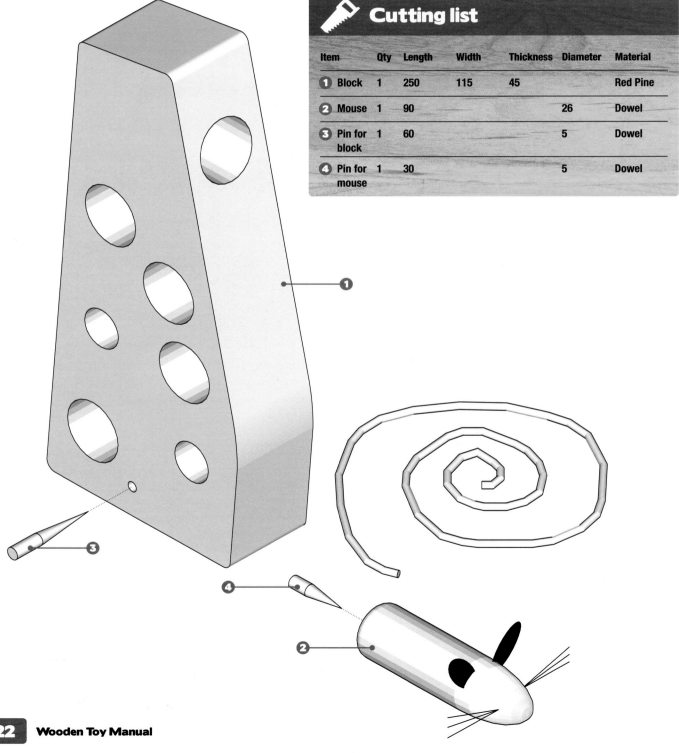

Cutting list

Item		Qty	Length	Width	Thickness	Diameter	Material
1	Block	1	250	115	45		Red Pine
2	Mouse	1	90			26	Dowel
3	Pin for block	1	60			5	Dowel
4	Pin for mouse	1	30			5	Dowel

1 Plotting out the holes to be drilled in a large chunk of timber, deciding where the small and large holes will be.

2 A large drill bit is used. Note the clamp on the Pillar Drill holding the wood safely in place.

3 A hole being drilled in the side of the block. It's always safer and easier to drill the holes before you shape the block.

4 The cheese block with different diameter holes is shaping up.

5 Once all the holes are bored a 'cheese wedge' shape is marked out on the block.

6 Cutting the block to shape using a tenon saw.

7 A piece of dowel rod is held in the vice and a small drum sander on a Dremel is used to shape the mouse's nose.

8 Drum sander is changed for a cutting wheel to create the mouse's mouth.

9 The cutting disc is changed for a drill bit to make the hole for the whiskers.

10 I cut bristles from a sweeping brush and threaded them through to form the mouse's whiskers.

11 The whiskers are held in place by dabs of glue from the electric glue gun and trimmed to shape.

12 A small reamer is now fitted to the Dremel, which is opening a hole to take the ears.

13 The hole is widened out to take a small piece of leather. A spot of 'hot glue' is dropped into the hole.

14 The leather ears are pushed into the holes. No particular shape is necessary here.

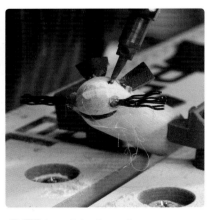

15 I used the Dremel VersaTip burner to make the eyes.

16 This mouse has a very, very long tail, which is fixed to the cheese block. Bore a hole in its rear end.

17 Now check that the shaped peg and string will go in.

18 Glue is now squirted into the hole and the cord with the peg is driven in.

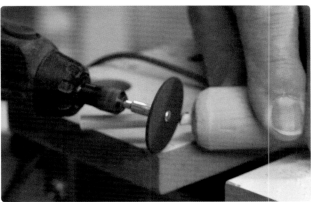

19 The cutting disc is used to cut off the peg excess. The other end of the tail is secured in the same way into the cheese block.

20 The VersaTip is used to blacken the cheese block and form a skin rind.

Pull-along train

This is one of those timeless toys that you just have to make. To keep it simple I've kept the timber to standard stock sizes. You can embellish this train, its carriages, station and signals as much as you wish, and the recipient will be chuffed to bits.

Pull-along train

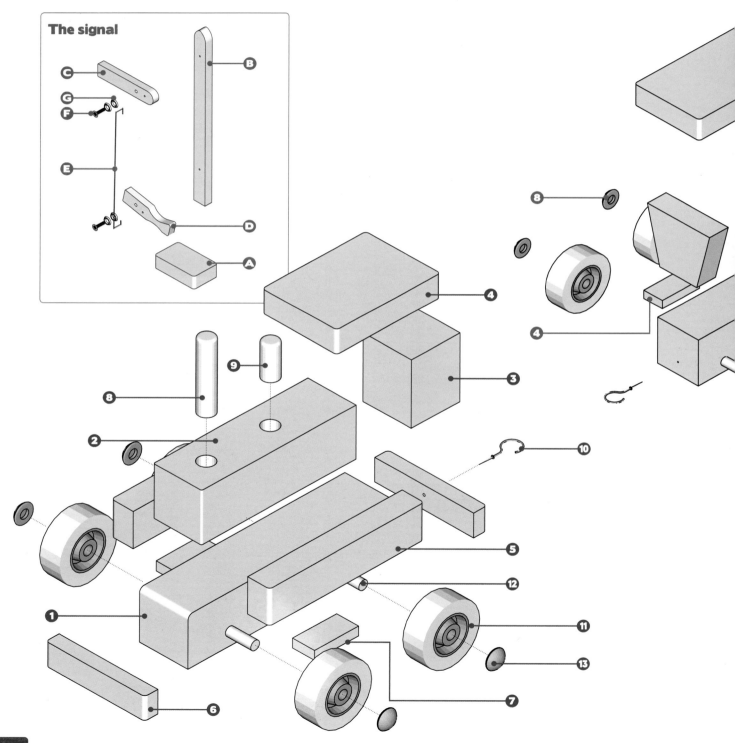

The signal

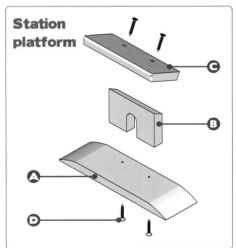

Station platform

![Cutting list icon] **Cutting list**

Carriage

Item		Qty	Length	Width	Thickness	Diameter	Material
1	Carriage Body	1	150	44	44		Red Pine
2	End Pieces	2	55	70	20		Red Pine
3	Roof	1	176	70	20		Red Pine
4	Runners	2	40	20	8		Red Pine
5	Hook	1					Brass
6	Wheels	4				48	Plastic
7	Axels	2	90			8	Steel
8	Hubs	4					Steel

Tank engine

Item		Qty	Length	Width	Thickness	Diameter	Material
1	Chasis	1	186	44	44		Red Pine
2	Boiler	1	140	44	44		Red Pine
3	Cab	1	56	44	44		Red Pine
4	Roof	1	94	68	20		Red Pine
5	Side panels	2	140	30	20		Red Pine
6	Bumpers	2	90	20	12		Red Pine
7	Steps	2	40	20	8		Red Pine
8	Chimney	1	62			14	Dowel
9	Steam dome	1	30			14	Dowel
10	Hook	1					Brass
11	Wheels	4				48	Plastic
12	Axels	2	90			8	Steel
13	Hubs	4					Steel

Signal

Item		Qty	Length	Width	Thickness	Diameter	Material
A	Base	1	70	42	20		Red Pine
B	Post	1	272	20	12		Red Pine
C	Signal arm	1	98	20	10		Red Pine
D	Handle	1	82	20	10		Red Pine
E	Wire	1					
F	Screws	2					
G	Screw cups	4					

Station platform

Item		Qty	Length	Width	Thickness	Diameter	Material
A	Platform	1	320	94	20		Red Pine
B	Building	1	136	90	24		Red Pine
C	Roof	2	204	92	20		Red Pine
D	Screws	4					

1 Mark out the body of the carriage. If you want very clean cuts mark over the pencil lines with a marking knife.

2 Cut to length using a tenon saw.

3 Pencil in the position for the axle holes.

4 The Pillar Drill is ideal for these holes, which need to be drilled accurately. Note the clamp holding the wood securely on the drill table.

5 One nice clean hole – repeat the operation at the other end.

6 Slip the axles in. I always use a drill slightly larger than the axle.

7 Slip the wheels on – just checking!

8 Marking out the ends of the carriage.

9 Cutting the tapered ends of the carriage with the Moto-Saw.

10 Applying the hot glue to the end.

11 Position the end, and press down hard – you have to be quick with the hot glue gun.

12 Using the Dremel Sander Band to round off the corners of the carriage roof.

13 Both ends are in place and glue is being applied to take the roof.

14 Press the roof down hard.

15 The steps are glued in place either side of the carriage.

16 A smooth-cut file is used to file a 55° angle on the end of the steel rod. This bevel allows the spring caps to be pushed on with finger pressure.

17 Spring caps fitted – never use a hammer on the spring caps.

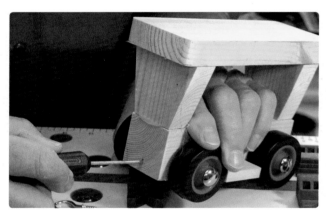

18 Use a bradawl to make a hole for the screw hook to be inserted.

19 Use a long threaded screw hook, as it goes into the end grain and we want it to be securely fixed.

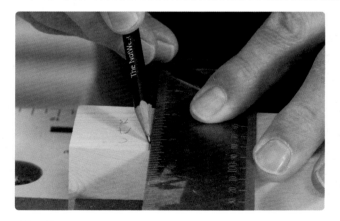

20 Making the engine is really a case of using the same technique as for the carriages. This is how it's done. Mark out the position for the cab.

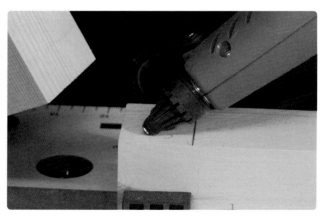

21 Now glue it into position.

22 The cab in place – note the position for the axle holes.

23 The loco body firmly clamped down for drilling of the axle holes.

24 The chassis with the axle holes drilled and the cab glued on. The boiler is next, a hole being necessary for the chimney and steam dome.

25 Holes being bored in the top of the boiler.

26 Two short lengths of dowel rod are prepared to form the steam dome and chimney. Chamfer the edges with the Dremel Sander Band.

27 Drop glue in the holes for steam dome and chimney.

28 A small hammer is used with a block of wood to drive the chimney and dome well into the prepared holes.

29 Just 'rounding off' the front of the chassis – little details like this are important.

30 Hot glue being applied to the chassis before mounting the boiler in place.

31 Boiler mounted in position.

32 Small strips of timber along the boiler sides to simulate tanks (this is a tank engine). The ends need rounding off.

33 Now hot glue the tanks on to the engine sides.

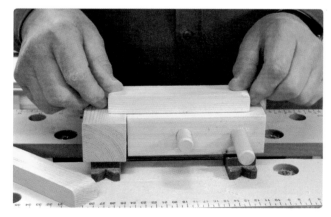

34 One tank in place. Now turn the engine over and fix the second tank.

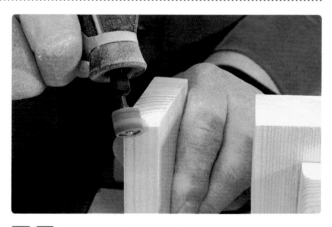

35 Now Dremel the cab roof to shape – remove all sharp corners and chamfer all the edges.

36 Hot glue the roof on.

37 Buffers are formed from two strips of wood, the ends being chamfered off.

38 The front buffer is glued in place.

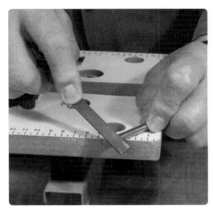

39 Don't forget to file the ends off the axle rods before trying to fit the spring caps.

40 The wheels in place.

41 The spring caps fitted.

42 A large screw hook being driven into the back of the engine, to be the towing hook.

43 Carriage and engine complete – all you have to do is to make more carriages.

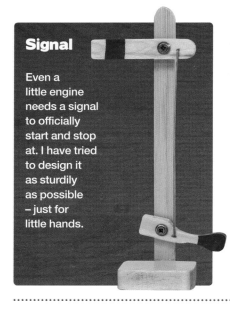

Signal

Even a little engine needs a signal to officially start and stop at. I have tried to design it as sturdily as possible – just for little hands.

44 The signal post is glued to a block of wood that forms the base.

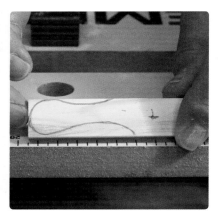

45 The signal lever is marked out in pencil.

46 The lever is cut to shape.

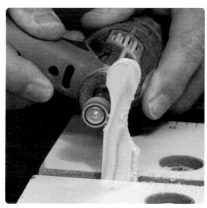

47 The Dremel Sander Band in action, shaping the lever.

48 Work all round the lever, taking chamfers off all the edges.

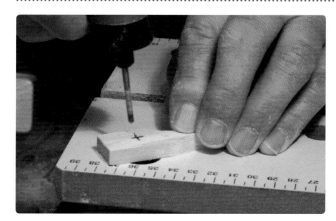

49 Now bore a small hole to take the screw that holds the lever to the signal post.

50 Very important – screw cups are in use here, as these form the ideal swivel point for a signal lever that's constantly being operated.

51 A screw cup is also used beneath the head of the fastening screw.

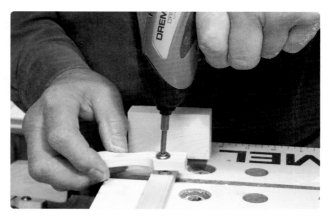

52 The lever is secured to the signal post. Don't do this up too tight.

53 At the top of the signal post the signal arm is attached using the same method, again with screw cups.

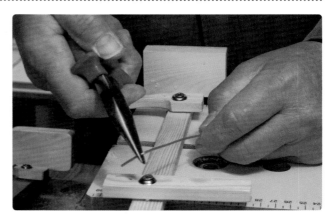

54 A length of stiff wire is shaped with a pair of pliers.

55 The wire is bent and fitted into a hole in the signal arm. The wire is then bent to fit the hole in the signal lever.

56 With wire in both holes of the arm and the lever, the signal should look like this.

Station platform

The only other essential ingredient is a simple station platform where the train can pull up to allow the passengers to board and alight.

57 A platform base is shaped up. The majority of the wood is planed away with a smoothing plane to form the required shape.

58 A battery-powered sander in use smoothing off the slope.

59 Marking an angle on the station wall that will take the roof. The angle is pencilled on both ends of the wall to provide you with a guide when you plane it.

60 A sharp plane is necessary for this task.

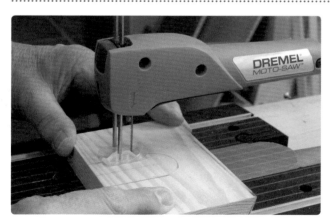

61 Sawing out the door in the station wall.

62 Using your Dremel, sand off the corners of the station roof.

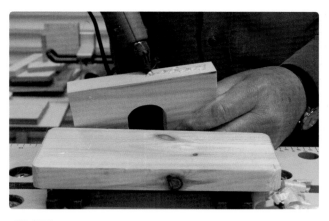

63 Use the hot glue gun to apply glue to the station wall.

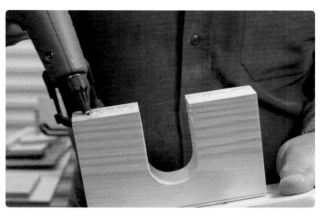

64 Glue is applied to the base of the wall also.

65 Fit the wall to the platform and pop the roof on – job done!

Woodpecker tree

I'm sure that you'll have seen such a woodpecker toy before. It's simple, and – as little things please little minds – timeless. I wanted to get my woodpecker not just to 'hop' down the tree, but to shake the pine cones off as he descended. A big woodpecker leaping down the tree will shake the dowel rod trunk and the tree above, the object being to shake off all the pine cones before he reaches the bottom.

Now, for some reason that I cannot fathom, some woodpeckers don't simply jiggle down the tree, they go round in a spiral as they descend – answers on a postcard to Haynes, please!

However, all this activity ensures that the pine cones come crashing off the tree. The cones need to be hanging on the dowel rods that have a downward slope – a touch of wax, and you'll have a toy that will amuse any young child.

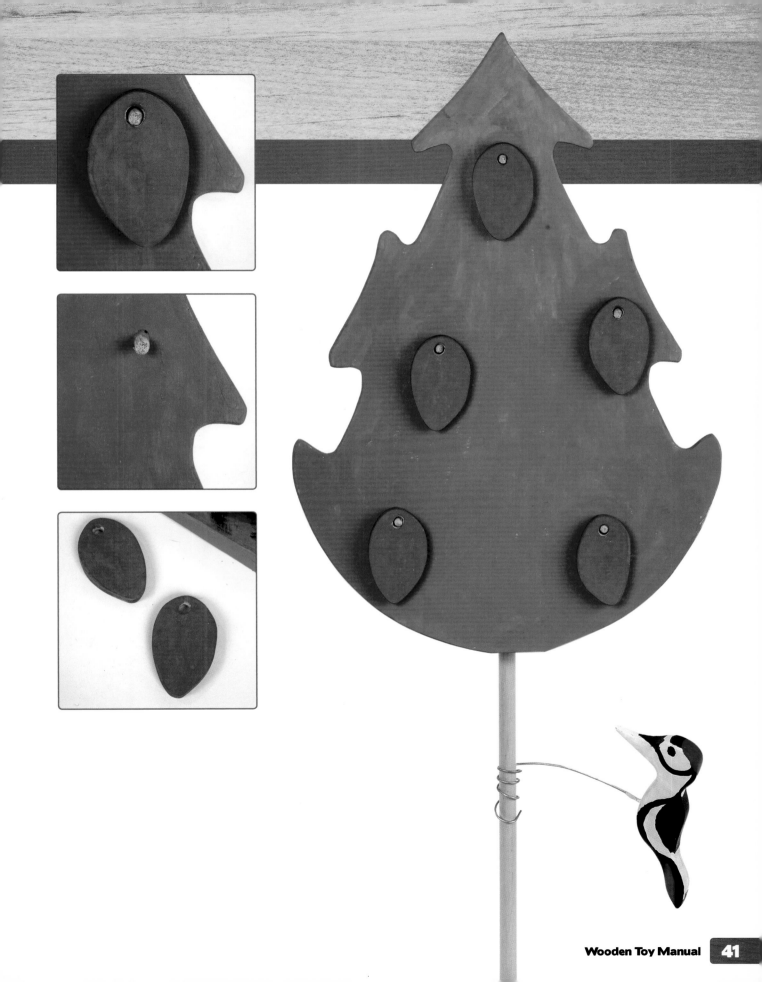

Woodpecker tree

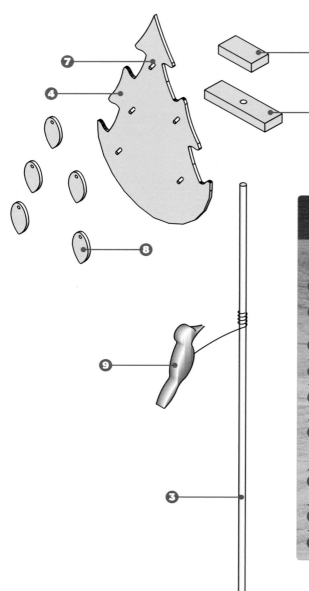

Cutting list

Item	Qty	Length	Width	Thickness	Diameter	Material
1 Base	1	220	140	20		Red Pine
2 Pole support	1	220	44	44		Red Pine
3 Pole (trunk)	1	1010			12	Dowel
4 Tree	1	460	300	6		Ply
5 Rear pole support	1	154	44	20		Red Pine
6 Rear pole support block	1	84	44	20		Red Pine
7 Dowel hooks	5	20			6	Dowel
8 Pine cones	5	70	40	6		Ply
9 Woodpecker	1	165	80	20		Red Pine

1 Mark out a very clear line on a sheet of plywood. The dark line makes it easy to see when you're cutting out.

2 Secure the plywood to the workstation with a clamp(s) and, cut along the pencil line.

3 The circular cutter on the Trio slices cleanly through the plywood.

4 If you veer off the line it's easy to have a second go at the cut.

5 Progress has been rapid, and the tree emerges from the surrounding plywood.

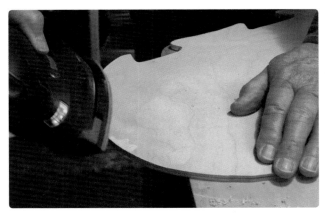 

6 I use the powered sander to tidy up the cut edges. Never leave sharp edges where little children are involved.

7 Mark out the holes for the dowel rods on which the pine cones will hang.

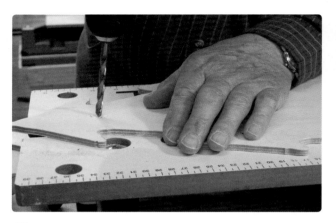

8 Drilling the holes – note the slight angle, which will help the cones to slip off more easily.

9 You can put more cones on the tree if you like, dependent on how many dowel rods you fix to the tree.

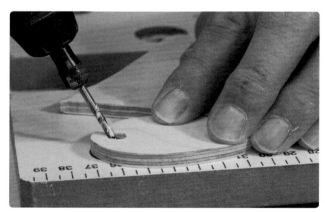

10 Glue the dowel rods into the tree – make sure that there's a downward slope as you push in the dowel rod.

11 A pine cone hole is enlarged with a drill bit or a Dremel bit.

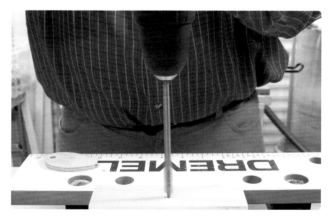

12 The top of the tree, with the cone about to be 'fitted'.

13 Using the drill/screwdriver to drill a large hole in a block of wood to hold the dowel rod 'trunk'.

14 Using the Dremel with a band-sander, slightly enlarge the hole to get the dowel rod to fit.

15 The dowel rod tree trunk is checked for fit into the base block of wood.

16 At the top of the trunk two pieces of wood are glued together. The first piece has a hole drilled to take the trunk, the second acts as a backstop for the drilled hole.

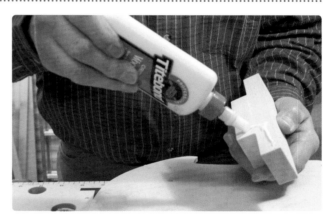

17 The glue is applied to both blocks which are positioned on the back of the tree.

18 Do a quick check to ensure that the dowel rod (trunk) fits the tree top end.

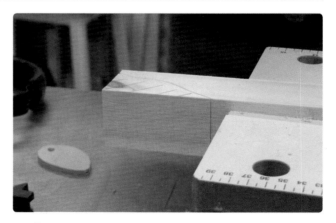

19 Back to the tree base that's been marked out ready for jigsawing into shape.

20 Cutting to shape with the jigsaw, the tree base being securely fixed in the vice.

21 Shaping up the tree base with the band-sander. All sharp edges and any saw cuts are removed.

22 The woodpecker is now cut to shape using the Dremel Moto-Saw. The saw cuts cleanly and leaves almost no saw cut marks.

23 Job done – a woodpecker is born!

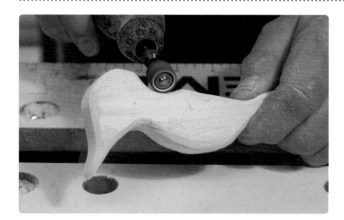

24 The Dremel carves/sands the woodpecker to shape – this really is as simple as it looks.

25 Stages of evolution: on the left the cut-out, middle the shaping under way, and on the right the completed bird, painted as a Great Spotted Woodpecker.

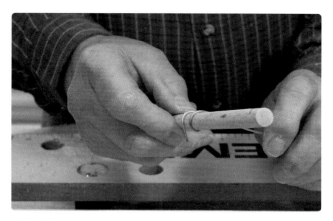

26 Take a length of fairly stout wire and wind it about four or five turns around a dowel rod, which must be the same diameter as the tree trunk.

27 Now drill a small hole in the woodpecker's chest...

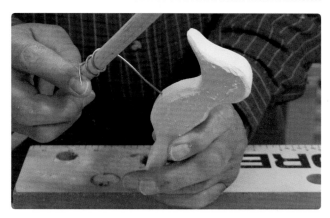

28 ...and push the wire in. It's a good idea to use superglue. Make sure the other end of the wire is wound to the diameter of the trunk. Now attach the woodpecker to his tree and see if he'll perform.

29 A bit of adjustment is usually necessary – uncoil the wire from around the trunk. You'll soon get the woodpecker jumping down the tree, with the pine cones falling all around!

Roundabout

As the roundabout is pulled or pushed along, one of its wheels turns the bottom disc and the centrifugal force spins the horses around and out. This toy is quite simple to make, but there are a lot of small pieces to cut out and assemble, which requires some degree of care and dexterity. The result is worth it though as the roundabout gives lots of pleasure.

Roundabout

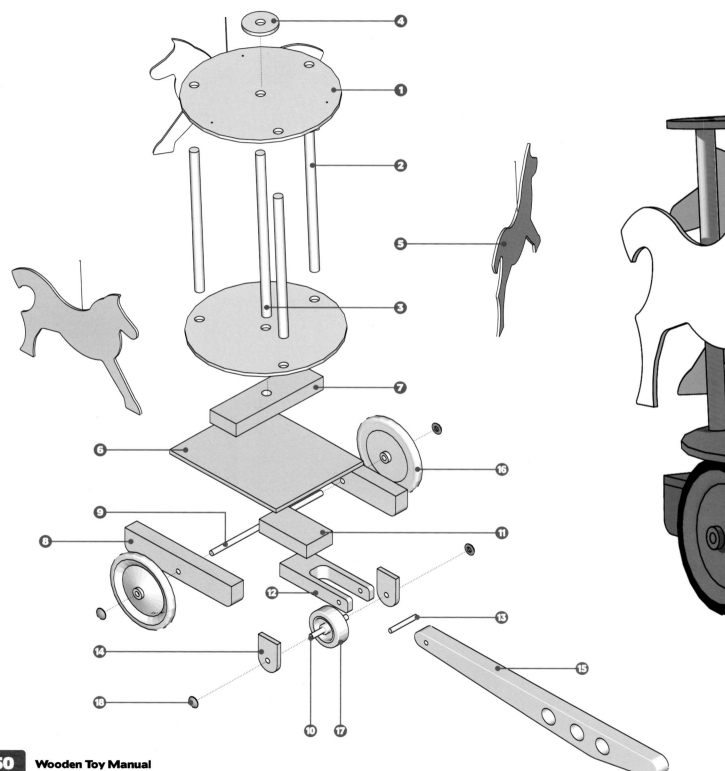

Cutting list

Item		Qty	Length	Width	Thickness	Diameter	Material
1	Top/bottom	2			6	194	Ply
2	Outer posts	3	220			12	Pine
3	Centre post	1	255			12	Dowel
4	Centre post top	1			6	45	Ply
5	Horse	3	230	200	3		Ply
6	Base	1	180	147	6		Ply
7	Support block	1	147	44	20		Pine
8	Side Bars	2	180	34	20		Pine
9	Rear axle	1	185			7	Steel
10	Front axle	1	60			7	Steel
11	Spacer block	1	80	44	20		Pine
12	Hinge block	1	115	44	20		Pine
13	Hinge dowel	1	44			6	Dowel
14	Front axle keeper	2	48	32	6		Ply
15	Handle	1	410	44	20		Pine
16	Rear wheel	2			15	105	Plastic/ Rubber
17	Front wheel	1			20	50	Plastic/ Rubber
18	Spring caps	4				16	Steel

1 As with all projects, you have to start by marking out. The chassis side members and base are the first to be made.

2 The two chassis side members are marked out and holes are drilled for the centre axle.

3 The axle is passed through the chassis side members.

4 The base of the roundabout is screwed to the chassis members.

5 Mark out the position for the dowel rod on the support block that will be glued to the base.

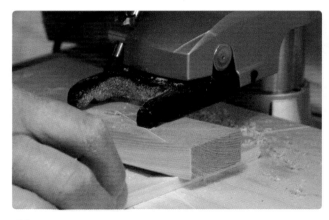

6 The dowel rod is offset at an angle – this is critical to the working of the roundabout. Note the small section of timber that's placed beneath the support block. When assembled the whole roundabout base rests on only one wheel, which allows it to rotate freely. The offset hole is now drilled. (Note the red lines in the photo are laser guides to assist with drilling.)

7 The dowel rod is inserted into the hole and the slight offset becomes apparent, though it's so small that it doesn't show up or spoil the look of the finished roundabout.

8 Glue the timber and position it on the base, making sure that the dowel rod viewed from above is in line with the axle rod beneath.

9 The chassis base and dowel rod all in position.

10 A small jockey wheel is fitted at the front of the roundabout. Note the axle rod ends have had a chamfer filed on them to facilitate the fitting of the spring caps.

11 The jockey wheel fits into the wooden yoke pictured, which the plywood keepers go either side of.

12 Pencil in the position for the axle hole.

13 Now drill the axle hole.

14 Cut out the front jockey wheel yoke.

15 Fit the wheel into the yoke.

16 Fit the plywood keepers, threading them on to the axle rod.

17 Wheel and plywood keepers assembled. Note the hole to take the pulling handle at the front.

18 Glue is applied to the block that mounts the jockey wheel to the chassis.

19 The jockey wheel plus the mounting block assembled.

20 The handle is marked up. I decided to decorate it with large holes drilled along its length.

21 Large holes being drilled in the handle. The handle is clamped firmly in place.

22 The handle is cut to shape. Some further finishing will be necessary to round off the edges.

23 The handle fits into the front of the jockey wheel.

24 By far the simplest way to produce the horses is to make a card template and transfer the shape on to thin plywood.

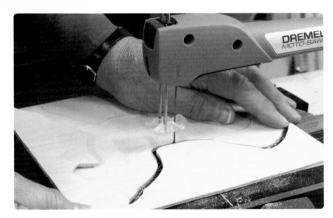

25 Cut out the shape of the horses from the plywood (you'll need three in total).

26 Having found the balance point, drill a small hole to take the nylon cord.

27 Now prepare the two discs that form the roundabout. Mark with a compass.

There are several different holes that have to be bored:

a) The centre hole around which the discs rotate;

b) The three holes that take the three outer supporting posts for the roundabout;

c) And in the top disc only, the small holes from which the horses are suspended.

For accuracy it's best to drill the discs together.

28 The large holes (for the dowel rods) have now all been drilled.

29 Making the small holes for the horses' suspension cords.

30 Hot-gluing the dowels into place.

31 The top disc is fitted.

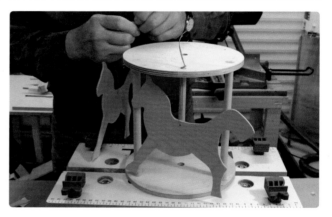

32 Horses being threaded on to the roundabout.

33 The jockey wheel assembly fits here...

34 ...and is now glued in place.

35 Turn the chassis over and fit the drive wheels.

36 The roundabout is now threaded on to the central dowel rod, and a check is made that the offset angle is sufficient for the disc to only touch one drive wheel. When you're satisfied, glue the central dowel rod in place.

37 A small circular disc of plywood is now glued on to the top to prevent the roundabout coming off.

38 A spring cap is pushed on to the axle. These clip on nicely, but only if you've filed a chamfer on to the ends of the axle rods. Don't be tempted to hammer them on – it won't work. Use the palms of your hands to press them on from either side.

Go-kart

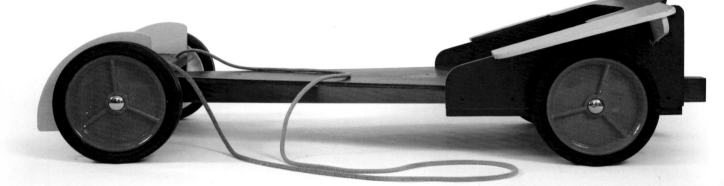

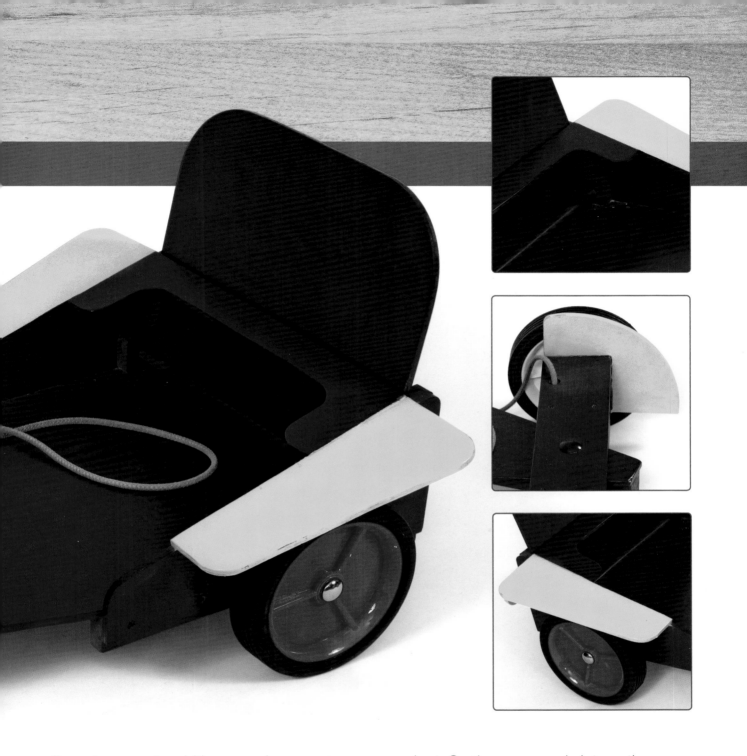

One of my great ambitions as a boy was to own a go-kart. Sorties were made into outhouses in search of wheels from old prams and pushchairs. The giant problem was to find four wheels of the same diameter, or at least two large ones for the back and a smaller pair for the front. My go-kart ambition wasn't achieved until I built one for my own children 30 years later.

Many go-karts have one big flaw: the front axle works loose and falls off. However, this go-kart has a split-axle and won't suffer from the embarrassment of 'losing your wheels'. Remember, this is a Haynes Manual, and Haynes know about these things!

Go-kart

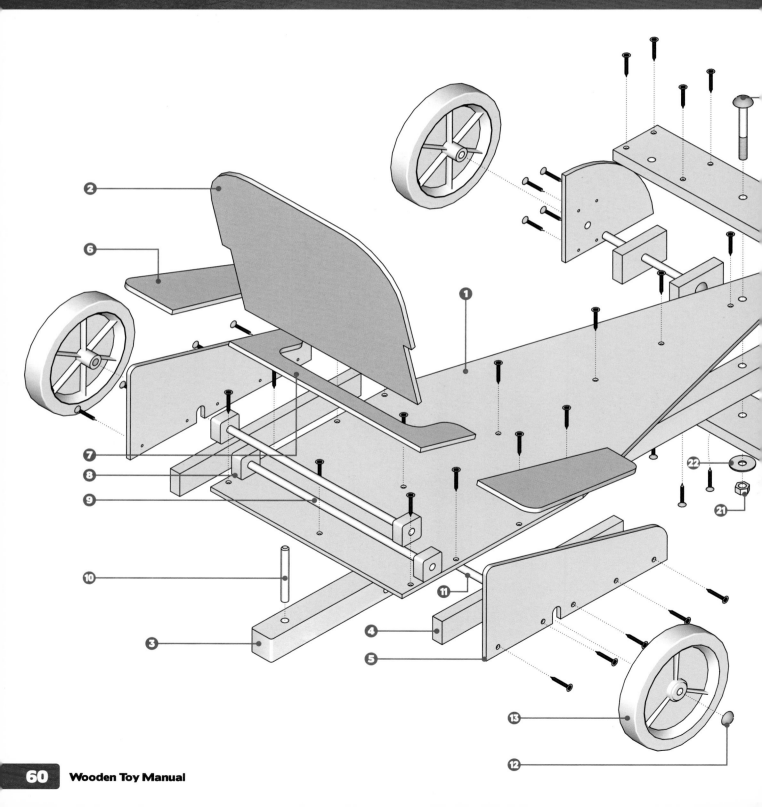

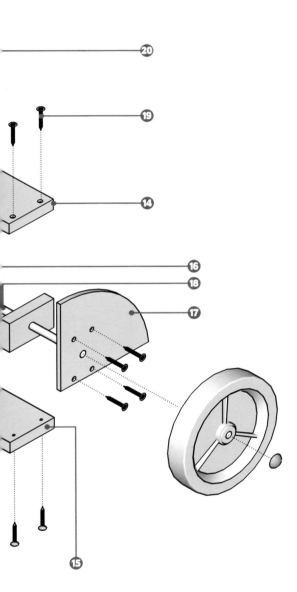

Cutting list

Kart body

Item		Qty	Length	Width	Thickness	Diameter	Material
1	Seat	1	1005	405	8		Ply
2	Back rest	1	400	330	8		Ply
3	Centre bar	1	1100	43	43		Red Pine
4	Side bar	2	382	20	43		Red Pine
5	Side panel	2	382	174	8		Ply
6	Mud guard	2	284	116	8		Ply
7	Back support	1	405	120	8		Ply
8	Block	4	40	40	20		Red Pine
9	Back support dowel	2	405			12	Dowel
10	Tow hitch dowel	1	100			12	Dowel
11	Rear axle	1	523			12	Steel
12	Axle caps	6				24	Steel
13	Wheel	4				200	Plastic/ Rubber

Front axle assembly

Item		Qty	Length	Width	Thickness	Diameter	Material
14	Top	1	456	94	20		Red Pine
15	Bottom	1	456	94	20		Red Pine
16	Spacers	4	94	54	20		Red Pine
17	End plates	2	186	164	8		Ply
18	Front split axle	2	207			12	Steel
19	Woodscrews	49					Steel
20	Bolt	1					Steel
21	Hex nut	1					Steel
22	Washer	1					Steel

1 The deck or platform of the kart is shaped from plywood. Ply is very strong and flexible and ideal for this purpose. Once marked out, the jigsaw is used to cut the shape.

2 Remember to fit a fine-tooth blade to prevent splinters. The platform/deck taking shape.

3 Down the middle of the deck, holes are drilled and countersunk to attach the centre bar beneath. This centre bar timber runs the full length of the kart.

4 Before attaching the centre bar to the deck, mark the position of the main back axle hole. Don't forget to drill a hole to take the tow hitch at the back.

5 Bore the axle hole. It's advisable to bore a hole just a little larger than the axle – this helps considerably on assembly.

6 Now drive screws through the deck into the centre bar beneath. Make sure the heads of the screws are well countersunk.

7 Now thread the axle through the centre bar.

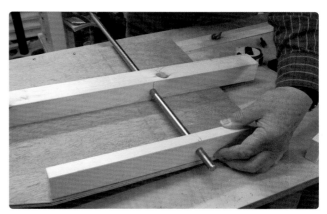

8 The axle is supported at the side of the deck by further timbers.

9 Both timbers in place, and the back axle supported at either end.

10 Turn the deck over and screw the axle supports in place.

11 Note the axle is kept in place while assembly continues.

12 A large 'flat bit' is used to drill the bolt hole for the front axle. It's best to buy the bolt first, which should be a goodly diameter.

13 It's very important to remove all sharp plywood edges along the side of the kart.

14 The sides are fitted and screwed to the kart. To make fitting them easier I cut a slot for the axle to fit in. This method allows for adjustment. Note the back axle showing clearly.

15 A panel at the back is now jigsawed to shape.

16 The shaped mud guards are now glued and screwed into place.

17 A mud guard being fitted, viewed from the inside.

18 The seat support is fitted.

19 Dowel rods with 'keeper blocks' on the ends are now screwed into place.

20 Clamp the 'keeper blocks' in place while the glue cures.

21 A second dowel rod and blocks is now glued in place on the deck.

22 The back rest simply slots into place between the two sets of dowel rods.

Front axle assembly

23 The front axle is made from six pieces of timber: four identical pieces to hold the axle and two timbers (one at the top and one at the bottom) to hold them all together – effectively a wooden sandwich! The four identical pieces in the 'sandwich' hold the axles. Prepare the four pieces of timber and bore holes in them to take the axle. Bore the holes slightly oversize. It's advisable to make up the axle blocks as pairs, and drill two at a time.

24 The front axle assembled, with the top section to be glued in place.

25 Now screw the top in place. Don't forget to add a drop of glue – it makes for a much stronger unit.

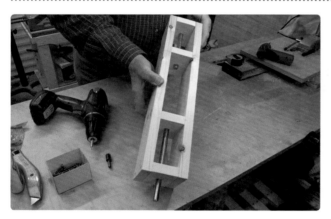

26 Slip one of the stub axles in and check that it goes into and through the second block. Use axle caps on the inner ends.

27 The front axle ready for the central bolt hole to be drilled. Mark up the position for the bolt hole.

28 The axle is clamped down securley and the bolt hole drilled.

29 Glue and screw the end plates on to the front axle to prevent shoes getting entangled with the wheels.

30 The coach bolt is fitted, with a nut and washer on the end.

31 Use a zinc-plated bolt – it won't rust. The front axle is fitted.

32 The wheels are fitted. The spring cap washers will only go on if you file a generous chamfer on the axle ends. Press the washers in place with your fingers or the palm of your hand.

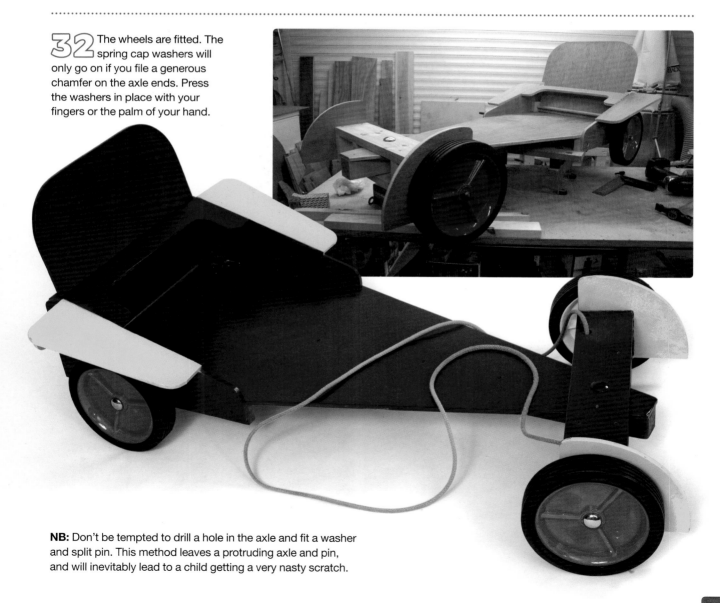

NB: Don't be tempted to drill a hole in the axle and fit a washer and split pin. This method leaves a protruding axle and pin, and will inevitably lead to a child getting a very nasty scratch.

Wheelbarrow

Twin-wheeled barrows are so much more stable than the single-wheeled ones. Consequently very young children will find this twin-wheeled barrow much simpler to use, as balancing the load is much easier. I've also arranged the wheels and axle centre to make tipping very simple. So if you want some help in the garden from your son or daughter, this is the project for you.

Wheelbarrow

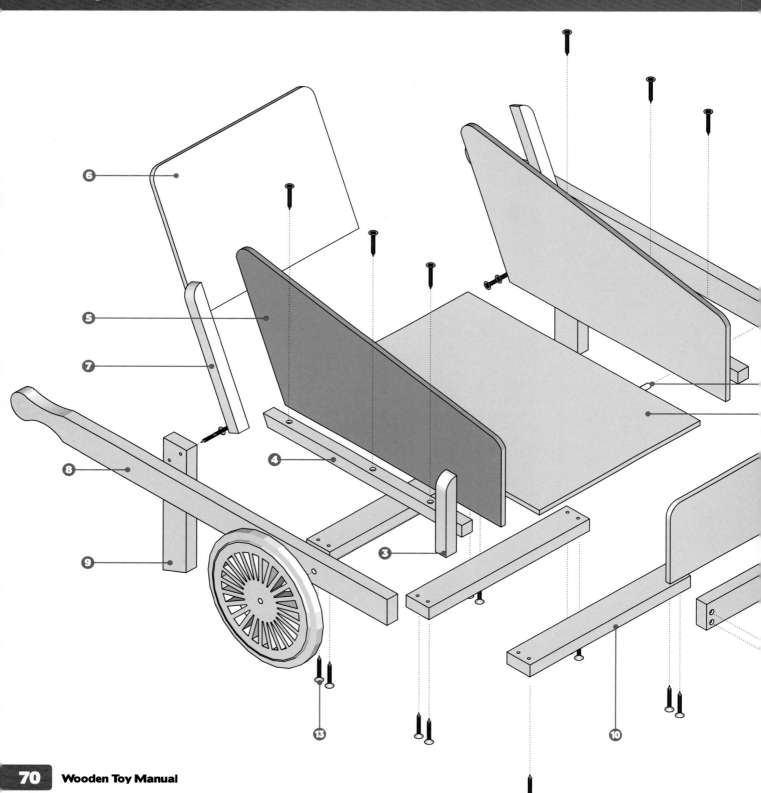

✂ Cutting list

Item		Qty	Length	Width	Thickness	Diameter	Material
①	Base	1	444	306	8		Ply
②	Front panel	1	306	130	8		Ply
③	Front supports	2	130	20	20		Red Pine
④	Lateral supports	2	380	20	20		Red Pine
⑤	Side panel	2	535	250	8		Ply
⑥	Rear panel	1	224	306	8		Ply
⑦	Rear supports	2	225	20	20		Ply
⑧	Chassis member	2	720	44	20		Red Pine
⑨	Legs	2	224	44	20		Red Pine
⑩	Cross member battens	4	306	44	20		Red Pine
⑪	Axle	1	309			8	Steel
⑫	Wheels	2			20	208	Plastic
⑬	Woodscrews	26					

1 Two battens are placed lengthways on the workstation, and the cross battens are positioned.

2 I actually use the batten with a carpenter's square to mark the place where the battens will be screwed to the chassis beneath.

3 Mark at one end the position for the axle hole.

4 At the other end pencil in the handle shape. This shape seems to fit snugly in a little hand.

5 It's a good idea to tape together both chassis pieces before drilling the axle hole.

6 With a fine blade in the jigsaw, cut the handle to shape.

7 The Dremel Sander Band is perfect for shaping the handle.

8 Now fit the axle through the two prepared holes.

9 Place a cross batten on to the chassis and check that it's 'square'.

10 Now position the other batten. Check with a carpenter's square that everything lines up.

11 A drop of glue beneath each batten comes next. Then the chassis is screwed together.

12 At the front of the chassis, a batten is screwed to the end. Since the screws go into the end grain it's worth slightly longer screws here. To prevent splitting, it's best to drill a small pilot hole first.

13 The barrow legs are now glued and screwed to the chassis.

14 The chassis together, complete with legs.

15 The plywood base is screwed to the chassis.

16 The task now begins of cutting out the panels that form the barrow sides and ends.

17 To make the barrow really strong for heavy loads, small strips of batten are screwed to the edges.

18 Glue is applied to the batten and screws are driven in. All the edges are treated in this way.

19 The panels are assembled for the 'box' body of the barrow. A clamp is very useful when positioning the edges prior to driving in the screws.

20 The end and side being screwed together.

21 The body is now screwed to the plywood base and into the chassis beneath. A small battery screwdriver is ideal for this job.

22 A close-up of the barrow body being attached to the chassis. Be sure to drive screws in right along the side, which will prevent the sides ever becoming detached from the chassis.

23 The end of the steel axle has been filed away to form a chamfer. The end caps are pushed on to the axle with the palm of your hand – they're excellent, and once fitted they won't come off.

NB: Since toy wheelbarrows are likely to get left outside, it's a good idea to use a wood preservative on them.

Market Stall

Playing 'shop' was always something that we did as children. We mimicked the adults. I remember an old cobbler's shop in the village, where besides the smell of leather there was the aroma of oranges. Why a cobbler should sell oranges I didn't question as a child, but I knew I'd remember it as one of those funny quirks of life in the country. Needless to say, our children's shop therefore had to have shoes and oranges for sale, much to my sister's disgust!

This toy is one of the 'easy' projects in this book, as long as you're proficient at folding a deckchair, because the construction is very much like a deckchair only wider. It therefore consists of a number of frames connected by coach bolts and nylon rope restraints.

Market Stall

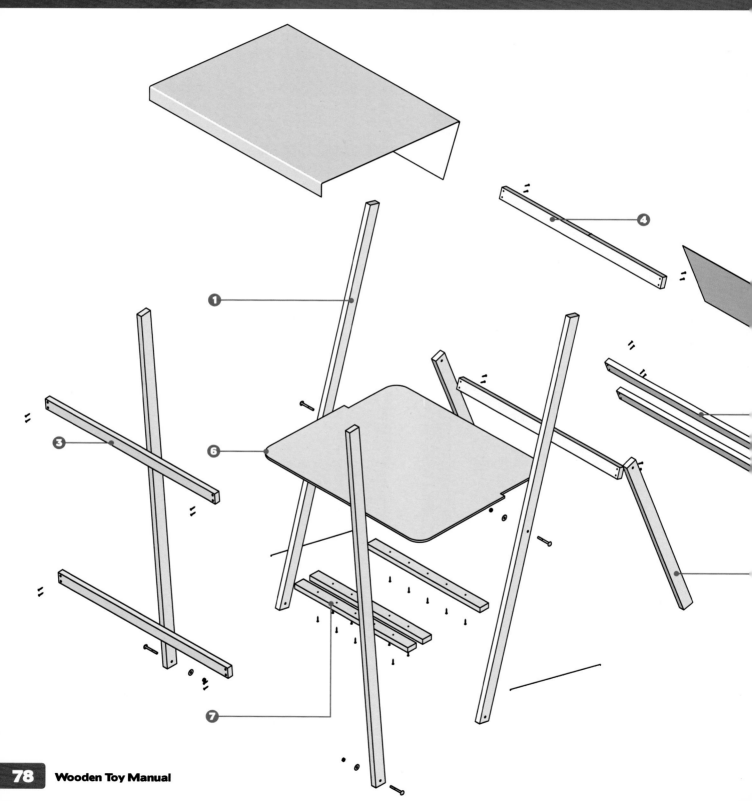

Cutting list

Item		Qty	Length	Width	Thickness	Diameter	Material
❶	Long upright	4	1520	40	20		Red Pine
❷	Short upright	2	760	40	20		Red Pine
❸	Cross battens (front)	2	780	40	20		Red Pine
❹	Cross battens (mid)	2	740	40	20		Red Pine
❺	Cross battens (back)	2	700	40	20		Red Pine
❻	Top	1	740	610	8		Ply
❼	Top supports	3	520	40	20		Red Pine

1 First you have to measure out the length of the legs for the front frame and its cross-timbers.

2 I use a bevel gauge to draw in the angle at the bottom of the legs.

3 Once the line has been pencilled in use a knife to cut the fibres – you'll then get a clean cut.

4 Mark all round the bottom of the leg.

5 Use a workstation or vice to hold the timber securely and then use a tenon saw to cut the angle.

6 Holes are bored at the top ends of the frame to take the coach bolts that attach it to the middle frame.

7 Before gluing in the cross-battens to form the frame use a smoothing plane to cut a small chamfer around all four edges of the leg. This chamfer prevents the grain being torn from the bottom of the leg.

8 Using the carpenter's square pressed against the cross-batten, mark on the legs where the cross-battens will be glued and screwed.

9 Holes are now bored at the bottom of the legs to take the nylon cord that limits how wide the front legs can be opened.

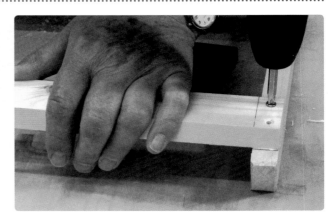

10 Screws are driven into the legs with the cross-battens.

11 The other side of the frame being screwed together.

12 Now you have lines pencilled in to show where the cross-battens go, but as you proceed you must use a square to check that the legs and battens are at 90° to each other.

13 Now work begins on the middle frame. It has a coach bolt hole at the bottom and two cross-battens – one near the middle (which acts as a shelf) and one at the top, which makes an attachment point for the vinyl cover.

14 Both legs of the middle frame are clamped together and the coach bolt holes are drilled (buy the bolts before selecting your drill bit).

15 Mark the position for the screw holes.

16 Now drill and countersink the holes.

17 This hole is for the coach bolt – it corresponds with the holes bored for coach bolts on the front frame.

18 Glue is applied...

19 ...the batten positioned...

20 ...and the screws driven in. Check with your carpenter's square that both timbers are at 90°.

21 The batten is screwed on. You can see beneath it the hole bored for the coach bolt.

22 An overall picture of the frame taking shape.

23 The third frame is made and the coach bolt hole is bored at the bottom of it. Both timbers are drilled together.

24 Cross-battens being screwed to the top of the third frame.

25 The middle cross-battens glued and screwed in place.

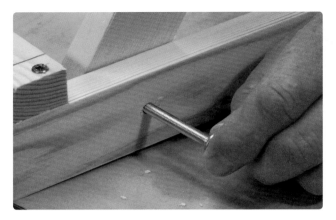

26 Coach bolt being fitted. Don't forget to slip a washer behind the nut before you tighten it up.

27 The front legs are restrained by lengths of nylon cord. The cord is threaded through the prepared holes. Tie a big knot on the end after you've threaded a washer on to the cord. The washer prevents the cord slipping through.

28 A piece of plywood with battens screwed beneath fits on to the cross-battens and forms the counter. The battens on the counter locate on to the spars.

29 The plywood counter is fitted and gives great stability to the whole framework.

30 A piece of thick vinyl cloth is stretched on to the top to form the canopy. A staple gun is a very effective tool for securing the vinyl.

31 The vinyl is extended below the counter – not structurally necessary, but it looks good.

32 The vinyl is wrapped around the front edge. I used yellow adhesive tape to add a touch of colour, and to cover the heads of the staples.

Tugboat

Children are unpredictable in what they say and do. They have great imaginations and can turn the simplest objects into things to be explored. A blanket thrown over a large cardboard box will become a den in the wilderness. An expensive tricycle taken out of its brightly coloured box is ignored and the child plays in the box instead! That's life.

I've designed this tugboat from a sheet of oil-tempered hardboard. With battens, screws and paint it shouldn't cost more than £10. If you're very lucky it might be sailed by pirates to attack a merchant ship, or abandoned in a raging gale, or attacked by sharks!

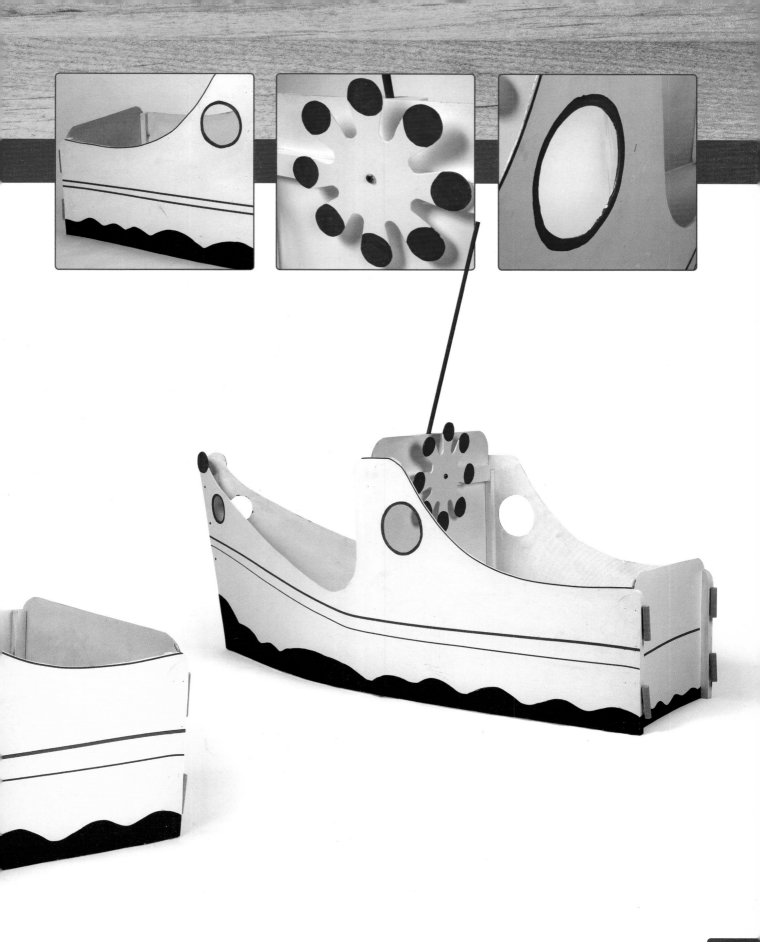

Tugboat

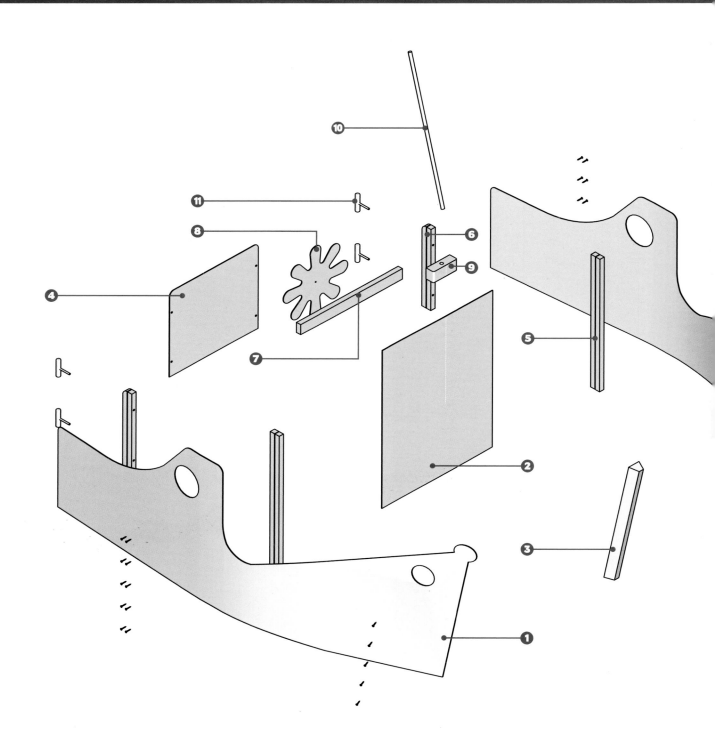

Item	Qty	Length	Width	Thickness	Diameter	Material
1 Side	2	1750	600	3		Oil tempered hardboard
2 Mid section	1	660	515	2		Ply
3 Bow support	1	530	50	50		Red Pine
4 Stern	1	415	360	2		Ply
5 Mid supports	4	560	20	20		Red Pine
6 Stern supports	4	340	20	20		Red Pine
7 Wheel support	1	475	44	20		Red Pine
8 Wheel	1			2	300	Ply
9 Mast support	1	110	44	35		
10 Mast	1	600			12	Dowel
11 Stern fastenings	4			70	12	Dowel

1 I used a plywood-cutting blade for this job. The most difficult thing to do is to support the sheet while you cut into it, as it tends to flop and bend. A large table is the best place to cut it.

2 Care has to be exercised, otherwise the board has a tendency to tear at the cuts if it's not supported throughout the cutting operation.

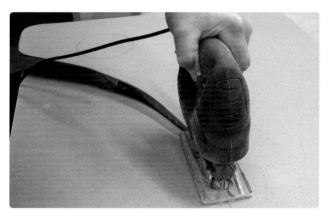

3 As you work around the board an extra pair of hands is useful.

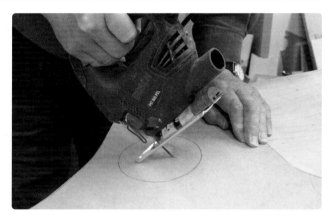

4 To cut the portholes you can either bore a hole to take the blade or do a sabre saw cut. The jigsaw is supported by its foot at the front, turned on and then very carefully rotated down into the wood.

5 Just rotate the jigsaw in the hole and cut the waste away.

6 To join the two halves of board together at the prow (front), I cut a batten of timber and then marked it out into a wedge shape. Pencil in the line to plane to very clearly.

7 Fixed in the workstation, planing begins. As you plane keep an eye on the two lines you've marked.

8 You'll end up with the batten resembling a wedge shape.

9 Drill and countersink the prow.

10 Fix the timber in the workstation and screw the prow of the boat to the wedge-shaped timber.

11 Now move to the back of the boat and drill and countersink holes.

12 Screw the side of the ship to the batten.

13 Now the back of the ship fits into two slots. I used an offcut of oil-tempered hardboard and clamped the second batten up to it. This gives the perfect dimension for the slot. Remove the scrap board and turn the ship side over.

14 Now screw the batten to the ship side.

15 Moving to the middle of the ship, pencil in where the battens go. Once again the middle section, like the back, just fits into a slot. The tension of the front and back being fixed keeps it in place – honest!

16 Now drill and countersink for fixing the battens.

17 Don't forget there are four battens to be fixed – two on the inside edge of each side.

18 The batten is visible here being screwed to the side of the boat. The battens are, of course, on the inside.

19 Screws are driven in all down the side. You'll need to check that the gap between the battens remains constant – check it with a piece of hardboard.

20 Now the prow of the ship is screwed together.

21 The back is fitted to the slot and screws are driven in. You can use dowel rods as pegs if you prefer – it makes dismantling and assembling quicker.

22 The middle of the boat is now fitted – the 'spring' in the board is sufficient to keep it in place.

23 A batten of timber has been fixed to take the ship's wheel. A block of wood is attached above this to take a dowel aerial.

24 I cut out the ships wheel from waste. Use screw cups beneath the wheel to get it to turn freely, not forgetting the screw cup beneath the screw head.

I painted the boat white. I then used blue paint to simulate the water. Finally I used red pinstripe tape to set off the white sides (this is available from motor shops, and is used to put stripes on cars and motorbikes).

Playhouse

This is one of those big projects that requires some knowledge of woodworking, plus the confidence to embark on such a large task. You also need to be able to lift and move wooden frames around, which can be very heavy when they're clad with shiplap planks. In addition it involves some expense, so it's sensible to look at the cost of the timber you'll need before you commit yourself.

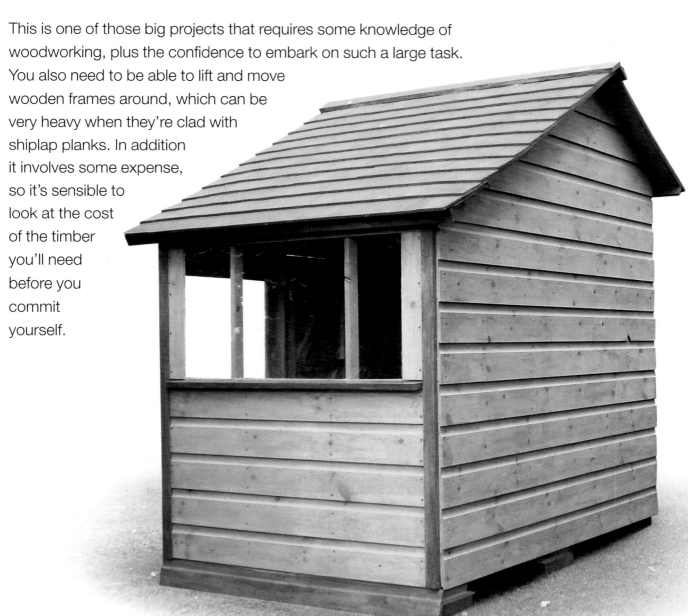

Playhouse

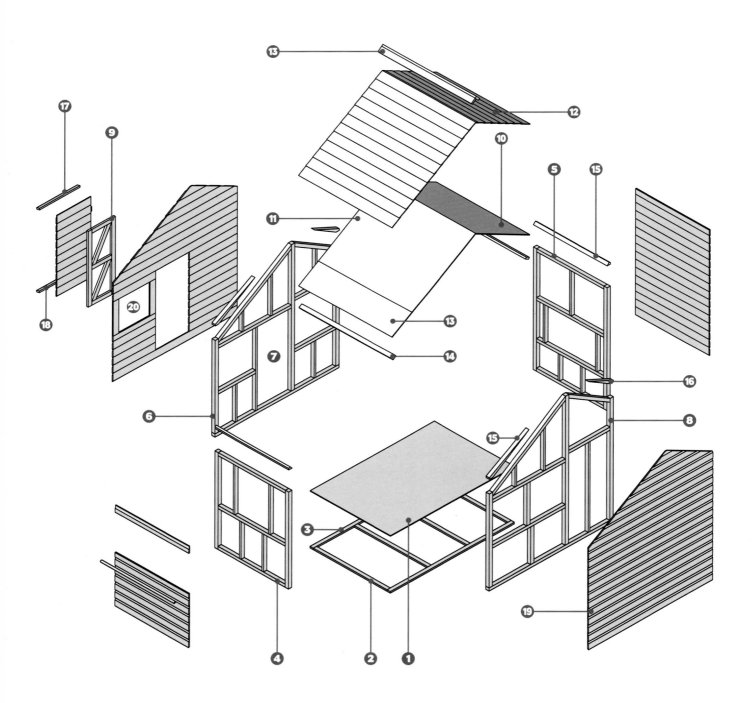

Item		Qty	Length	Width	Height	Thickness	Material
1	Base/floor	1	1830	1220		9	ply
2	Base batten	4	1120	50		50	pine
3	Base batten	2	1830	50		50	pine
4	Side frame A	1		1120	1220	50	pine batten
5	Side frame B	1		1120	1570	50	pine batten
6	Side frame C	1	1830		1830	50	pine batten
7	Doorway	1		500	1100		
8	Side frame D	1	1830		1830	50	pine batten
9	Door frame	1		430	1070	50	pine batten
10	Roof section 1	1		1440	900	18	ply
11	Roof section 2	1		1440	1300	18	ply
12	Shingles		var	var			cedar
13	Capping boards	2	1440	90		20	pine
14	Roof board	2	1440	60		20	pine
15	Tapered batten	2	750	50		0–25	pine
16	Tapered batten	2	500	50		0–25	pine
17	Door ledge	1	600	70		25	pine
18	Door rain bar	1	500	50		50	pine
19	Cladding		var	var		var	ship lap
20	Windows						Perspex

I tend always to build things that will last, so all the framework is 50mm square; the addition of a wooden shingle roof is an extra expense, but it does look good. The other advantage of building your own playhouse is that you can build into the framework the necessary supports for bunk beds etc. Although the height is sufficient for two bunks, the length is a little restricted – but it's possible.

The use of shiplap boards makes it very easy to clad the wooden frames. The glazing is Perspex, so there will be no danger of broken glass.

Many of the projects in this book can be made with a good selection of hand tools – jigsaws, Dremel tools etc. However, for this project a battery screwdriver is essential, and so is a compound mitre saw. Even at their most basic these tools cross-cut timber very accurately. The majority have the ability to cut the timber at a huge variety of angles, while some can cut compound mitre joints, and the 'big daddies' of the range can manage all this plus full cross-cutting of wide boards.

The essential element in all this is that in order to create wooden frames, the timbers used must be cut at their ends to exactly 90° in both planes. You may be skilled with your hand saw, but you'll never compete with the mitre saw for accuracy and speed. These machines can be hired, but I suspect that once you've experienced their agility and accuracy you'll have to have one – you have been warned!

1 The cross cut is made in a piece of 50mm timber – the same dimension as is used for framing the playhouse.

2 If you're jointing timber at the corners you want to avoid splitting the wood. Large, long screws are necessary. Bore pilot holes for the screws.

3 Use a countersink so that the heads are below the surface – you don't want projecting screw heads.

4 An example of driving a screw into a corresponding piece of timber to form a 90° joint. Note just how well both timbers go together. Without these accurate cuts you'll find it difficult to use this method of framing to build the house.

5 These are some of the most valuable pieces of kit you'll need all the time: an expanding rule, large square, waterproof glue, an ample supply of screws and a battery screwdriver are all essential.

6 The floor must be square, otherwise the house just won't join up at the corners. Use the sheet of plywood that's square to ensure that the battens are screwed on to its edges.

7 Frequently the plywood will not lie flat until fixed. Screw and glue the floor to the timbers beneath. A couple of clamps are very useful.

8 The timbers that make up the frames need to be measured with care. When assembly begins the outside frames will go on the outer edges and these frames will be on the inside. Note the 'gap' left on the bottom left-hand corner to accommodate the side frame. Check the measurements here. The end frames fit inside the side frames.

9 The ship lap board goes on the outside of the frame. The first board to be fixed goes at the bottom of the frame. The shiplap board is normally extended about 30mm below the bottom of the frame. When floor and frame are assembled this overlap ensures that water cannot enter the house.

10 The door end with the shiplap being screwed in place. When you come to an opening it's a simple job to cut the shiplap down to fit.

11 The door is simply a framework covered with shiplap board. Note the braces fitted in the door.

12 Inside looking out. The door opening is to the right, the window to the left. Although all the main framing is in 50mm x 50mm, note the 50mm x 25mm that's also used. This lighter timber gives you a fixing for the shiplap on the outside and provides a good fixing point for the board.

13 I assembled the house for a 'dry run' and to measure the overhang I wanted for the plywood roof. I like generous overhangs on buildings – it looks better than a 'short back and sides'. The picture shows the windowsill, which needs to be angled downwards to shed the rain. Note that the top window board has been planed down to accommodate the angle of the roof.

14 Using Canadian white shingles is a bit of a luxury, but it gives the house a wonderful 'woody' look, besides being more attractive than the felt roof which is the alternative. Tile bales come in a variety of sizes. Select the sizes as you go along, and make sure that you overlap the tiles. I used a compressed-air nailer to fix the tiles. You can use a large industrial stapler, but if you do you'll probably have a sore hand at the end of the day. All the fixings are totally hidden, as they're covered by the overlapping tile above.

15 Floor down, one end and one side fitted. I used a clamp on the corners, which is sufficient to hold things together. Note the bottom left-hand corner – the end leaves room for the side. I designed this house for two short bunks to be fitted. The frame on the right-hand side is designed to take what will be the timbers of the bunk beds. The top bunk has reduced headroom.

16 The same stage from a different angle. When the other sides are added will be the time to screw the ends to the sides. These screws need to go right through the frame of one side and well into the frame of the other. It's also advisable to screw the sides to the floor. It's a good idea to leave the final screwing together until all the sides are on the floor. This allows some 'jiggle room' for adjustment.

17 I made a capping board for the roof. The roof is screwed to the sides and the capping board screwed to the roof.

The door catch needs to be on the inside – a catch or bolt on the outside will leave the imaginative little dears the opportunity to turn it into a prison!

A good quality wood preservative should be used, and all the edges treated. Finally, fit the Perspex. I simply used clear acrylic caulk, which worked extremely well. The caulk is applied all around the edges of the Perspex. This is very effective and has so far survived one autumn and winter without showing any sign of movement.

Rocking elephant

The rocking horse has always been the most popular of wooden toys. Over the years I've seen designs for rocking horses that would win the Cheltenham Gold Cup if given the chance, and at the other end of the scale simple plywood-bodied horses – Shetland pony style.

But I thought that I'd make a rocking elephant instead. Over 30 years ago I made one for my daughter, which she still has and loves. So here, for another generation of children, is the design for my rocking elephant. Though the 'bodywork' only requires cutting from plywood, the rockers are a bit more traditional in construction – but nothing that time, patience and a good jigsaw won't achieve.

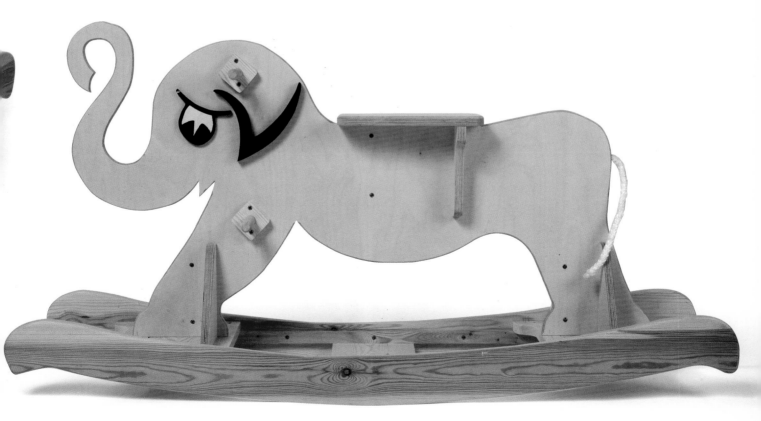

Rocking elephant

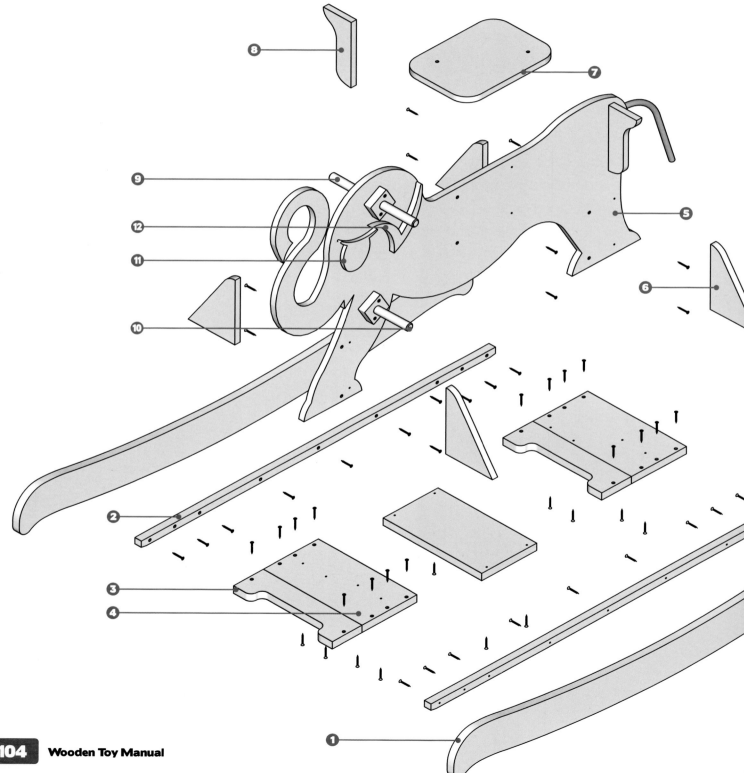

Cutting list

Item		Qty	Length	Width	Thickness	Diameter	Material
1	Rocker	2	1370	150	20		Red Pine
2	Runners	2	1070	20	20		Red Pine
3	Shaped cross pieces	2	300	90	20		Red Pine
4	Cross pieces	3	300	166	20		Red Pine
5	Elephant shape	1	1070	630	18		Ply
6	Supports	4	180	142	18		Ply
7	Seat	1	280	200	18		Ply
8	Seat supports	2	180	85	18		Ply
9	Handle/footrest	2	256			20	Dowel
10	Handle/footrest supports	4	55	55	20		Red Pine
11	Eye shape	2	115	90	10		Ply
12	Ear shape	2	160	125	18		Ply

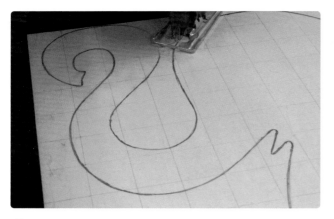

1 Having heavily pencilled in the shape of the elephant on 18mm plywood, the next task is to cut it out.

2 It's essential to use a fine-cut blade in order to cut cleanly without leaving those ugly splinters that are the norm when you try to cut plywood.

3 The blade must also be sufficiently thin to go round the curves of the trunk. This is a fairly thick plywood, so don't rush it. If the blade is right, the jigsaw will cut steadily and cleanly, and you don't have to run the machine at full speed.

4 One of the simplest mistakes while cutting, particularly on curves, is a tendency to push sideways instead of forward. The blade then bends, and the cut surface isn't 90° if measured from the face of the board.

5 The trunk emerges from the sheet of plywood. The offcuts will be used later. The trunk around the elephant's head is the most difficult part to cut. The legs and body are less intricate.

6 The Dremel Trio is fitted with a router cutter that not only removes the 90° edge but also nicely 'rounds off' the plywood. It's a good machine for this job, and totally controllable.

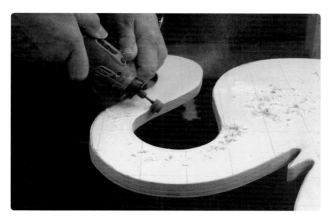

7 The other tool for the job is the 'old faithful' sander band. Work over the whole elephant body, making sure that there are no splinters or sharp surfaces that a child can get snagged on.

8 The jigsaw is the perfect tool for cutting rockers. The fine-cutting plywood blade is removed and a standard wood blade used.

9 Rocking horses, particularly Victorian ones, had large, beautifully shaped bow rockers, and the horse rocked like a Grand National winner. However, this isn't relevant for a rocking elephant, so these rockers are 'bowed' for a sedate rock.or safety's sake I've designed a reverse curve on the end of the rockers. This helps prevent any chance of the elephant rocking right over.

10 Note that it's important to select knot-free timber for these – a knot could be a possible weak point where a break might occur, so select the timber carefully.

11 The jigsaw is so adept at cutting shapes – the secret is to keep the body of the jigsaw turning when approaching a curved line and make no sudden deviations in direction.

12 Remember to remove the sharp edges.

13 A battery-powered sander is used to finish off. I like to get a neatly well-turned edge on the rockers – they look so much better with this shaping.

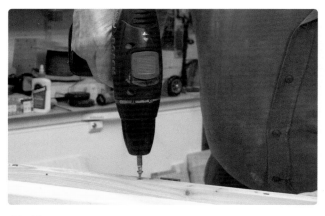

14 On to the inside edge of both rockers a batten rail is screwed along its entire length. This rail becomes the fixing point for the platform on which the elephant sits.

15 The offcuts from cutting out the body shape are now used to form triangles. These triangles will sit on the platforms and are screwed and glued in place. The advantage of the 18mm plywood is that it will take large screws.

16 It's best to drill small pilot holes for the screws, which will prevent any chance of splitting the ply – although this is unlikely with such a thick ply.

17 Here the triangle is being held firmly to the elephant's front leg and a screw is being driven in from the other side.

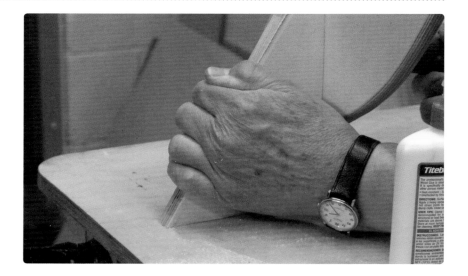

18 On this side one triangle has been fitted. The triangle on the other side is offset. The screws securing it are being driven in.

19 The seat is made from another offcut (top of the picture). A plywood bracket has been secured by screws from the other side. The bracket for the other side is being screwed in place. The brackets are offset. The seat is screwed from the top into the brackets.

20 The handle is made from a large dowel rod, and square plywood 'washers' are shaped and screwed in position. The purpose of these 'washers' is to increase the gluing area and make the handle a much stronger fixture.

21 The footrest is fixed, glued and screwed to the elephant body. If you only bore a hole and glue in the dowel rod it will certainly work loose, hence the plywood washers.

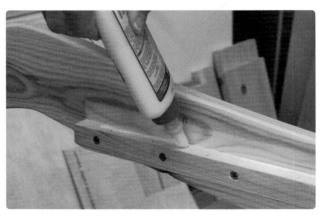

22 Both rockers are held together by lengths of timber which are screwed to the longitudinal rail that runs the full length of the rockers.

23 Glue is applied, which with the screws makes for a very strong joint.

24 Platforms are screwed at the front and the back. It's important to get good fixings because a rocking toy takes a great deal of strain.

25 The platform at the back being fixed. Note the shape of the rocker. The 'reverse curve' is shown, which acts as a brake on the rocking toy.

26 The elephant is placed on the platform, the position of the triangular 'stands' marked, and holes bored from the top side. Getting someone to hold the elephant, turn the whole unit on its side and drive screws through the platform base into the triangular blocks attached to the elephant.

27 Once the first two screws are fixed it's far simpler to complete the job, but the extra pair of hands at this stage is invaluable.

28 Now bore a hole in the back of the elephant and glue a length of rope in. It's a good idea to sharpen the end of a small dowel rod and drive it in with the glue. The dowel will act as a wedge and help prevent the tail being pulled out.

29 The eyes and ears I cut from scrap ply. Paint them black. The eyes and ears are far more prominent if you make them like this.

30 Either use self-adhesive sticking pads to secure the eyes and ears, or glue them direct on to the elephant's head.

31 One jumbo toy worth all the effort, will give hours and hours of fun.

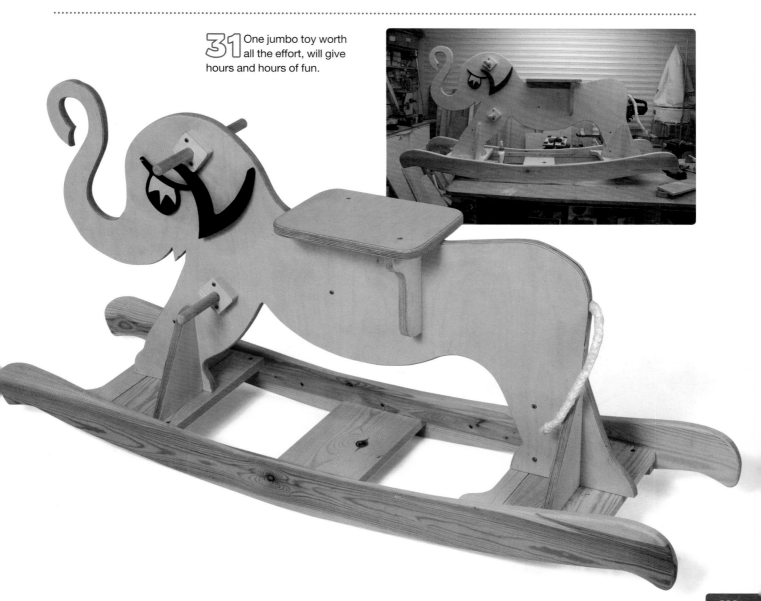

Trike & trailer

Difficulty

Youngsters never seem to tire of scooting along on a wheeled trike – away they go, legs going like pistons, and no L plates! Mobility is of tremendous importance to children, especially if they have a trailer full of goodies to cart around!

Trike & trailer

Project components

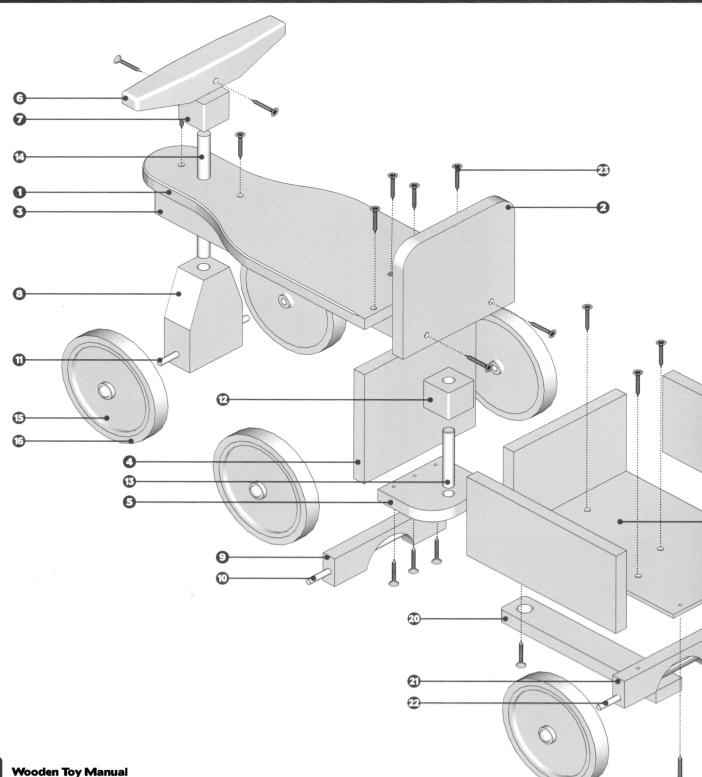

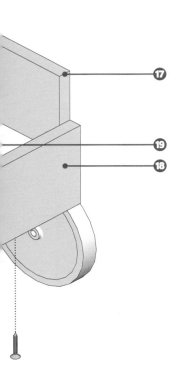

✂ Cutting list

Trike

Item	Qty	Length	Width	Thickness	Diameter	Material
1 Seat	1	455	190	18		Ply
2 Back	1	176	190	18		Ply
3 Centre bar	1	418	44	40		Red Pine
4 Lower back	1	180	190	18		Ply
5 Tow hitch	1	92	107	18		Ply
6 Handle bars	1	255	44	40		Red Pine
7 Steering spacer block	1	44	44	44		Red Pine
8 Front axle block	1	140	90	44		Red Pine
9 Rear axle block	1	190	45	20		Red Pine
10 Rear axle	1	260			8	Steel
11 Front axle						
12 Tow hitch spacer block						
13 Tow hitch dowel	1	90			15	Dowel
14 Steering dowel	1	240			15	Dowel
15 Wheel	6		22		140	
16 Tyre	6		22		10	

Trailer

Item	Qty	Length	Width	Thickness	Diameter	Material
17 Side panel	2	255	126	18		Red Pine
18 End panel	2	192	126	18		Red Pine
19 Base	1	255	192	6		Ply
20 Tow bar	1	268	44	20		Dowel
21 Axle block	1	192	44	20		Red Pine
22 Axle	1	260			8	Steel
23 Woodscrews	31					

1 Never start a project without carefully marking it all out in pencil. When it's marked out, check it all and then work over the job in your mind, checking where the pieces will go. This is guaranteed to save both frayed tempers and timber!

2 The seat is the first candidate to be marked up. A nice generous curve at the front end is ideal. Here the hole for the front steering arm is being pencilled in.

3 Plywood cuts cleanly if you use the correct blades, otherwise you'll have wood splinters everywhere, and it spoils the finish. This blade is fine-toothed, made by Bosch (No T101A0, so now you have no excuses!).

4 These fine blades are very sharp. Don't push the jigsaw hard – it will cut superbly with a gentle even pressure.

5 All the edges of the trike seat need to be carefully rounded off, otherwise the legs of a child will become sore. This rounding off can be done in a number of ways – palm sander, router or this shaper/router table which the Dremel slots into enabling you to control the cut throughout the whole operation.

6 A quick final finish with one of the band-sanders.

7 Holes are bored in the trike seat to take the back and the centre spar that forms the backbone of this toy. Note the drill has a countersink bit attached. It's vital to countersink all the screws, otherwise the screw heads will scratch.

8 The centre bar timber is now screwed and glued to the seat.

9 A large hole is bored to take the steering rod. Note the clamp has been removed for the picture – clamps must be fixed before drilling begins.

10 Use some fairly lengthy screws at this point. You may need to drill pilot holes for these. Some modern screws will both draw the parts together and not split the plywood.

11 To get a really good joint here I used a clamp to hold the parts together while driving in the screws.

12 The back seat is screwed to the trike.

13 A block is required to carry the steel axle. The axle hole is marked up carefully from both ends.

14 The standard drill lengths aren't sufficient to go right through the block. Instead both ends have to be drilled. Particular attention is paid to keeping the drill at 90° in both planes. I use a carpenter's square on the vice to help me do this. If you have a Pillar Drill it's simple, but this hand and eye method requires more skill.

15 Now cut the middle of the axle out and it removes the blank piece in the middle where the drill can't reach.

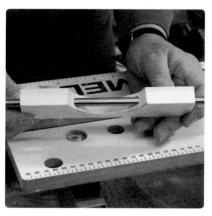

16 Thread the steel axle into place.

17 The back axle is now both glued and screwed into position.

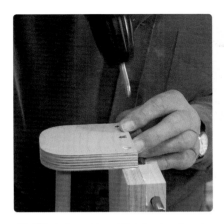

18 A dowel tow hitch is glued and screwed to the back of the trike – I can't imagine a trike without a trailer!

19 The hitch firmly in place.

20 A steering handle is now shaped up. The underside is cut to shape with a tenon saw.

21 A battery-powered sander is used to make a smooth, beautifully shaped handle.

22 Work around all the edges.

23 Now bore the hole to take the dowel rod that actuates the steering.

24 The front axle is a stout chunk of wood – bore a hole for the axle.

25 Drive the dowel rod into the axle block. Some resistance may well be felt as the dowel rod meets the glue.

26 Cut and fit a wooden spacer.

27 Squirt glue into the prepared hole in the steering handle.

28 Fit the steering handle.

29 Fit the wheels.

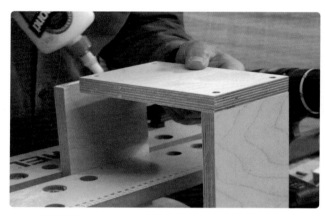

30 The trailer is in effect a simple box made from plywood. Apply glue to all the edges...

31 ...and screw the box together.

32 The base is made from plywood. Glue is applied...

33 ...and the base screwed in place.

34 An axle block is made for the trailer in exactly the same way as for the trike. The axle block and the tow bar are screwed to the plywood base of the trailer.

35 The axle is in place.

36 Now fit the wheels. Don't forget to prepare the axle ends by filing a chamfer on them. Then, using hand/palm pressure, fit the wheels on to the axle ends – never use a hammer.

Pull-along trolley

Go-karts, wheelbarrows and trolleys – all things with wheels appear to have a fascination for youngsters. Helping in the garden requires a barrow, or just pulling a trolley along with the flowerpots and potting compost – all very engrossing stuff for youngsters. The trolley is designed to be used either as a flat-bed, or by slotting the cage body on it can be filled with sacks, pots and tools etc.

Pull-along trolley

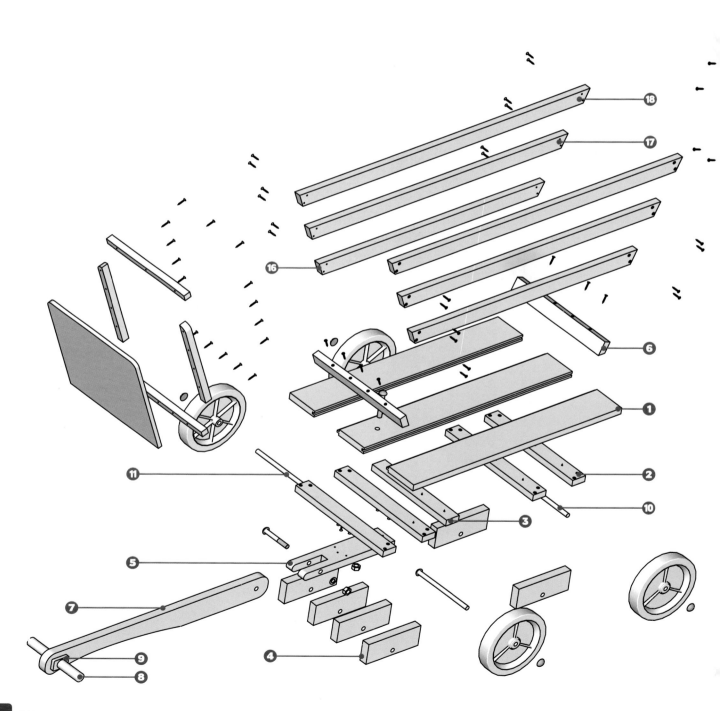

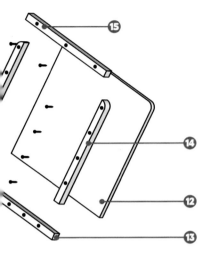

⚒ Cutting list

Item		Qty	Length	Width	Thickness	Diameter	Material
1	Top slats	3	710	100	20		Red Pine
2	Axel cross pieces	4	354	44	20		Red Pine
3	Top cross piece	1	300	44	20		Red Pine
4	Axel supports	6	178	68	24		Red Pine
5	Handle bracket	1	310	70	24		Red Pine
6	Box end supports	2	354	44	20		Red Pine
7	Handle arm	1	760	70	24		Red Pine
8	Handle	1	200			26	Dowel
9	Handle mountings	2	50	34	10		Ply
10	Rear axel	1	448			12	Steel
11	Front axel	2	200			12	Steel
12	End pieces	2	364	354	12		Ply
13	Bottom end bracket	2	354	20	20		Red Pine
14	Side end brackets	4	344	20	20		Red Pine
15	Top end bracket	2	314	20	20		Red Pine
16	Bottom side strut	2	770	44	20		Red Pine
17	Middle side strut	2	884	44	20		Red Pine
18	Top side strut	2	992	44	20		Red Pine

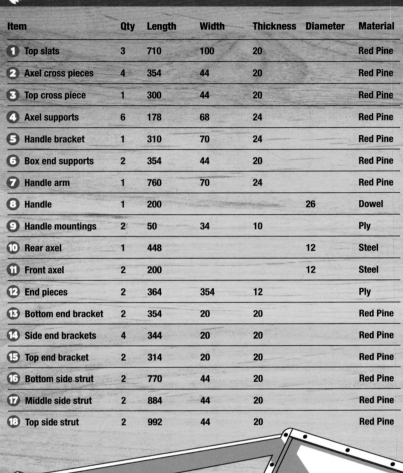

1 How many of you look at objects and wonder if they might have a secondary use? Tongued and grooved floorboards fit into this category for me, hence I've used them for the trolley bed. Prepare the boards by planing off the groove on one side and the tongue on the other, and you have a base.

2 The three boards that form the bed, with the groove and tongue removed on the outer edges.

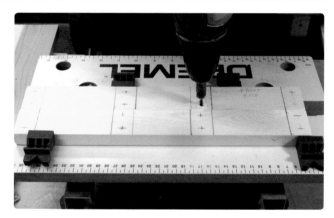

3 Now you need to make the front axle, so mark out in pencil where the axle supports will go.

4 Drill and countersink the holes on both sections of the timber.

5 These four pieces of timber are all exactly the size needed to be sandwiched between the timbers you've already marked out. Before you do this, the axle hole has to be bored. I taped the timbers together and then clamped them to the Pillar Drill table and drilled the holes. Cut the tape off and you have a pack of axle blocks – repeat for the other two.

6 A pair of axle blocks, the holes bored and the axle in place.

7 Assemble the unit.

8 Now it's time to make the tow hitch. The hitch provides an anchorage point for the handle and is fixed to the front axle. Bore a hole to accommodate the bolt that will hold the handle.

9 Now drill and countersink the holes that attach it to the front axle.

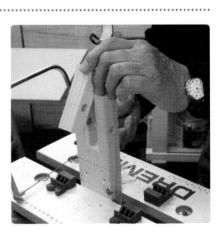

10 A slot has to be cut in the tow hitch to take the handle. Cut down the sides with a tenon saw.

11 Now here's an old favourite – just in case you think that I've forgotten how to use hand tools, a coping saw is used to cut out the waste.

12 Now glue and screw the front axle components together. As you do this make sure that the tow hitch fits snugly between the two inner axle blocks.

13 The tow hitch is now fitted to the front axle.

14 The front axle complete and assembled.

15 Now work begins on the back axle. This is really a repeat of the front axle, with the inner axle blocks and tow hitch missing.

16 Don't forget to glue as well as screw the unit together.

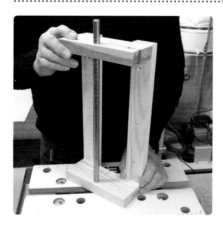

17 The back axle complete.

18 Bore a hole in the deck to take the front axle bolt.

19 The bolt is inserted into the deck.

20 The front axle is positioned over it.

21 A washer is placed beneath the nut before it's tightened up.

22 A batten of timber is screwed behind the front axle to keep the tongued and grooved planks together.

23 The back axle is now screwed on to the deck. This not only holds the axle unit to the deck but also keeps the tongued and grooved boards together.

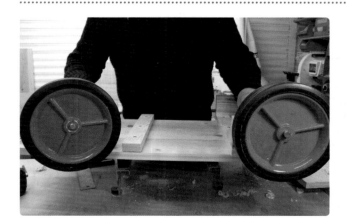

24 Now pop the wheels on just to see that it all works. It's always encouraging to put the wheels on – it feels as if you're getting somewhere!

25 The handle of the cart has a nice big dowel rod handle. However, dowels just stuck into a handle always work loose, so to prevent this a large plywood-type 'washer' is made.

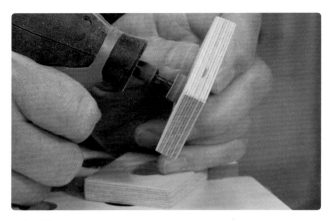

26 A Sander Band is used to enlarge the hole, giving the dowel rod a good fit but allowing for plenty of glue to get into and around the joint.

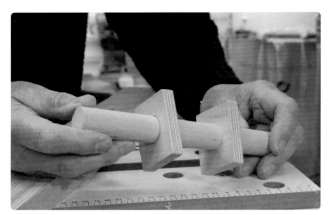

27 This is the dowel and the plywood 'washers'. The other advantage of such plywood washers is that they enlarge the gluing area available and make for a very strong handle.

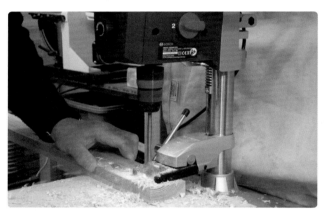

28 Now work begins on the handle itself. Bore the hole to take the dowel rod.

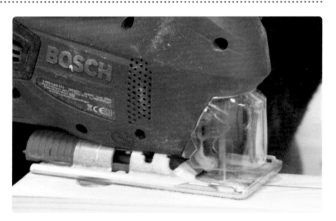

29 Now jigsaw the handle to shape.

30 Remove the saw cut marks and generally curve the handle to a nice smooth shape.

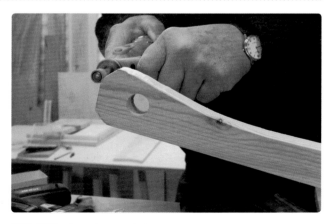

31 The 'roughed out' shape is quickly smoothed.

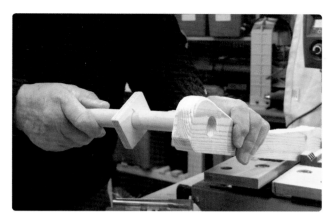

32 Do a 'dry run' to try the dowel rod in the handle before you use glue, otherwise if it won't fit first time things become very messy.

33 Gluing the dowel handle in place.

34 Apply a couple of clamps to the plywood 'washers' to make a good, tight bond.

35 A coach bolt is fitted into the tow hitch and handle.

36 A washer is placed beneath the nut before tightening up.

37 The cart top is made from plywood ends, with battens holding the ends together. The plywood ends are edged with strips of wood. This is a necessity, as it gives the battens holding the ends together a good screw anchorage point.

38 One of the ends nearing completion.

39 The tops of the ends are rounded off. It's important that all sharp corners are removed.

40 The first of the battens holding the ends in place is fixed.

41 Batten fixing goes on apace.

42 You can see clearly how the timber edgings that were screwed on to the plywood ends now provide strong and vital anchorage points for the battens.

43 One of the features of the cart is that the top can be removed rapidly. To achieve this, two shaped lengths of timber are screwed to the top of the deck.

44 Before screwing them into place an angle is planed on the bottom of the batten. This angle compliments the angle given to the plywood ends of the top.

45 The angle of the batten is important for a good fit. A little patience with a smoothing plane (a sharp one) will achieve this.

46 Fitting the top to the cart.

47 Job done – now, who's gone off with my wheels?

Pirate ship

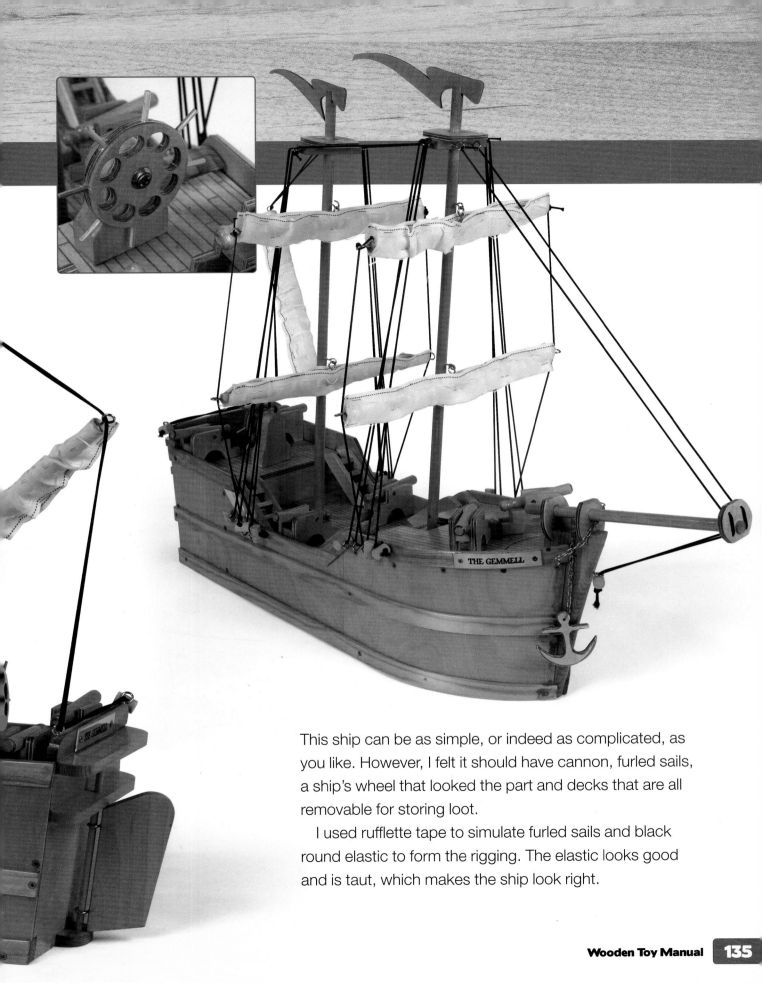

This ship can be as simple, or indeed as complicated, as you like. However, I felt it should have cannon, furled sails, a ship's wheel that looked the part and decks that are all removable for storing loot.

I used rufflette tape to simulate furled sails and black round elastic to form the rigging. The elastic looks good and is taut, which makes the ship look right.

Pirate ship

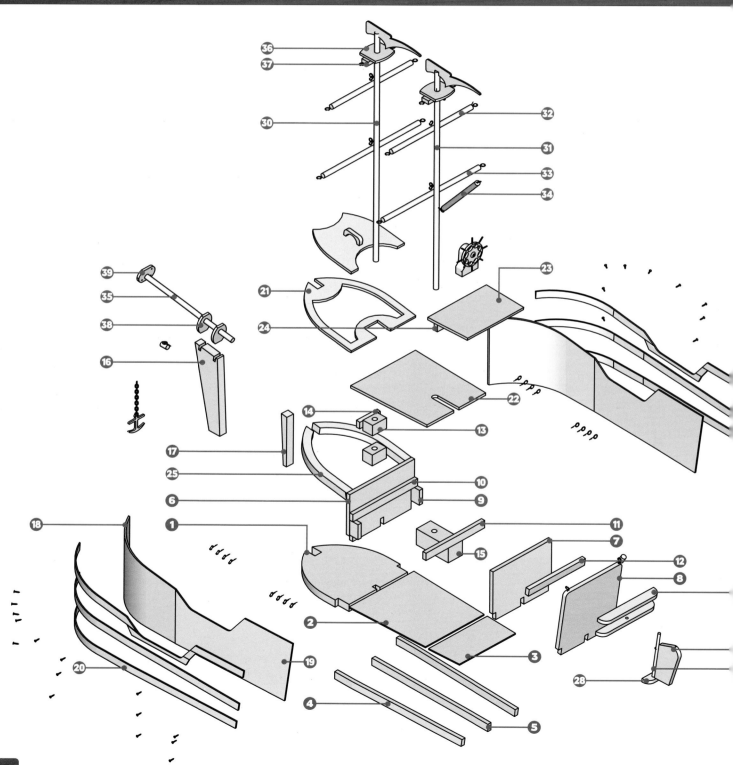

Cutting list

Item		Qty	Length	Width	Thickness	Diameter	Material
1	Fore section base	1	220	203	20		Red pine
2	Mid section base	1	230	202	3		Ply
3	Aft section base	1	93	183	3		Ply
4	Side support	2	387	20	10		Red pine
5	Centre support	1	364	20	10		Red pine
6	Fore bulkhead	1	202	20	10		Ply
7	Mid bulkhead	1	202	134	10		Ply
8	Aft bulkhead	1	175	190	10		Ply
9	Side reinforcement blocks	2	41	26	10		Ply
10	Forward mid deck support	1	202	20	10		Red pine
11	Rear mid deck support	1	183	20	10		Red pine
12	Rear aft deck support	1	175	20	10		Red pine
13	Fore mast support blocks	2	44	30	30		Red pine
14	Fore deck support	1	64	20	10		Red pine
15	Mid mast support	1	100	44	44		Red pine
16	Bow stem	1	230	70	20		Red pine
17	Bow stem support	1	140	20	16		Red pine
18	Fore hull	2	300	186	4		Ply
19	Aft hull	2	338	172	4		Ply
20	Hull reinforcements	6	638	20	3		Ply
21	Fore deck incl. hatch	1	231	202	7		Ply
22	Mid deck	1	230	202	7		Ply
23	Aft deck	1	122	183	7		Ply
24	Forward aft deck support	1	181	20	10		Red pine
25	Fore deck side supports	2	260	20	20		Red pine
26	Rudder	1	126	60	10		Red pine
27	Rudder supports	2	175	24	10		Red pine
28	Rudder base	1	50	20	10		Red pine
29	Rudder rod	1	135			6	Dowel
30	Fore mast	1	640			12	Dowel
31	Mid mast	1	610			12	Dowel
32	Upper boom	2	250			12	Dowel
33	Lower boom	2	300			12	Dowel
34	Aft boom	1	300			12	Dowel
35	Jib boom	1	280			12	Dowel
36	Crow's nests	2	60	60	6		Ply
37	Supports	2	75	20	10		Red pine
38	Jib boom supports	2	50	40	6		Ply
39	Jib boom end piece	1	50	35	6		Ply

1 The shape of the prow is best formed by making a cardboard template and then transferring the shape on to plywood.

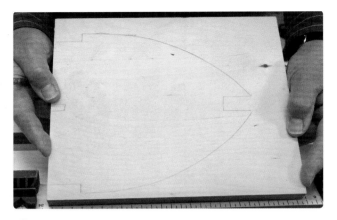

2 The marked-out prow ready for cutting out.

3 Make a start cutting out the shape. Take your time and let the blade do the work – don't force it.

4 The centre support is fitted.

5 The side supports are screwed into the side.

6 A little glue is also applied.

7 The second side is screwed in place.

8 Overview of the keel and the basic frame of the ship.

9 The main prow timber is shaped.

10 A great deal of timber can be removed with a 'milling cutter'. You can curve the prow timber rapidly to shape with this.

11 The prow timber is now hot-glued into place.

12 The middle bulkhead is fitted. Note the prepared blocks of wood with holes drilled to take the mast.

13 The stern is fitted. The fillet of timber on the inside edge is to support the deck.

14 The prow of the ship ready to receive the curved deck timbers.

15 The curved deck timbers being cut to shape on the saw.

16 The timber is screwed to the prow.

17 The plywood is fitted to make the bottom of the ship – there are three sections like this.

18 The ship on its side, with plywood being screwed in place. Plywood is bent and screwed along the sides of the hull. The most difficult part of the job is getting the first screw fixed.

19 The second fixing is at the bottom – once these screws are secure it's comparatively easy to continue down the side of the ship.

20 Screwing the plywood down at the stern.

21 Gluing in the block holding the second mast. It's glued to the second bulkhead, and goes beneath the strip of timber that's glued to the bulkhead.

22 Mast and block in place against the bulkhead.

23 The rear section of the ship.

24 The front decking is now cut to shape.

25 Fixings for the jib boom are fitted.

26 The jib boom fitted.

27 Middle deck is fitted. **NB:** For clarity, one side of the ship hasn't been fitted.

28 Rear decking being positioned.

29 The piece of timber being fitted here holds the bottom of the tiller.

30 The tiller rod is glued into position.

31 The tiller is fitted. Small screw eyes have been used to attach the tiller to the rod.

32 Glue is applied to the top bar that holds the top of the tiller bar.

33 The bar is fitted and the tiller secured.

34 Glue is applied to the mast and a very basic 'crow's nest' is pushed up into the glue.

35 The timber beneath the platform has screw eyes attached for the rigging.

36 Rufflette tape is stapled to dowel rods to simulate furled sails.

37 A screw eye is fixed in the middle of the sail and a screw hook fixed to the mast.

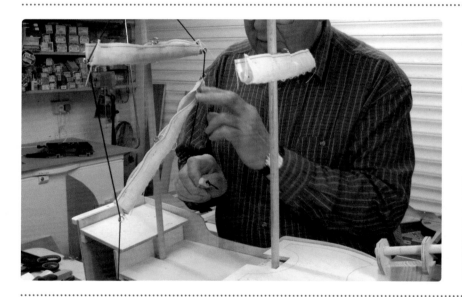

38 Sail being assembled and fitted to the mast.

39 I used short lengths of dowel rod, drilled with holes, to form toggles. The elastic was threaded through and knotted to the toggle. Screw hooks then formed the anchorage point for all the rigging.

40 The cannon. First mark out the cannon's carriage.

41 Cut the carriage to shape with the saw.

42 Take a length of dowel rod and pencil a line approximately 12mm from one end.

43 Now using a band sander, work a groove into the dowel rod. When finished it will look like the end of a cannon.

44 At the other end chamfer off the mouth of the cannon. If you use a high speed you can create a black line around the cannon mouth.

45 Returning to the cannon carriage, glue a piece of timber on to one of the carriage sides – repeat on the other side.

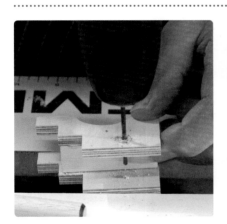

46 Bore a hole right through the carriage side and into the second side.

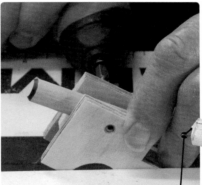

47 Hold the carriage in the vice – offer up the cannon and drive a screw from both sides into the cannon.

48 The finished gun looks like this and the screws through the carriage sides allow the elevation of the gun to be altered.

This is one of those lovely toys that I can only call an evergreen – it falls into the same category as a doll's house, fort/castle and rocking horse. Today there are some beautiful scale models of tractors, balers, ploughs, Land Rovers and so on to dress the farm with. The farm itself can be as large or indeed as intricate as you wish. You can have a little farm with pig sheds, hen houses and horse stables or go the other way with implement sheds for tractors and a combine harvester. Whichever you choose, it's nice to see a plywood base for the farm to be assembled on, or even better with a green baize (railway model shops sell this) covering the ground, with a few splodges of mud (railway shops again). This approach makes it look very realistic.

Farmyard

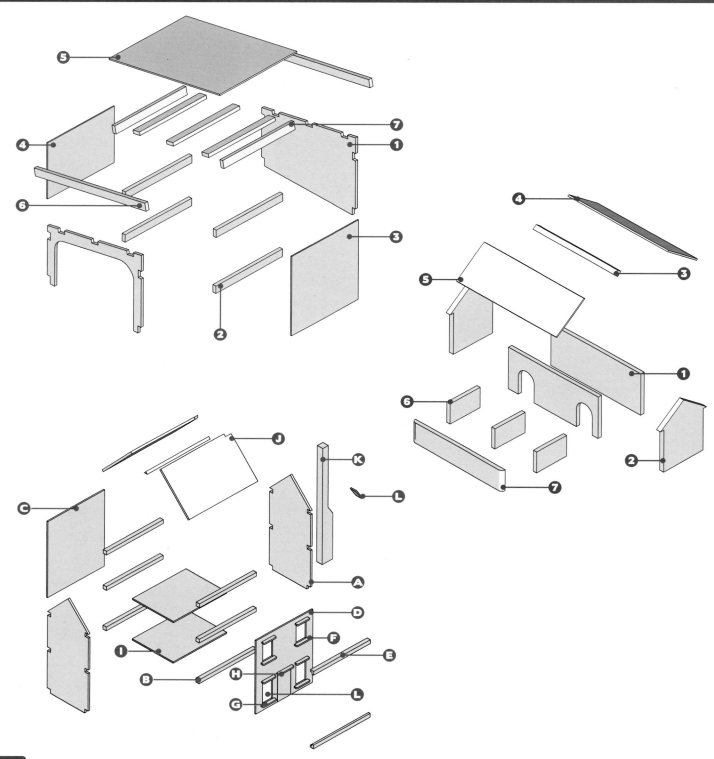

Dutch barn

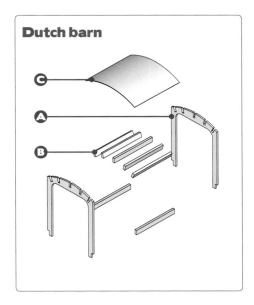

Stable

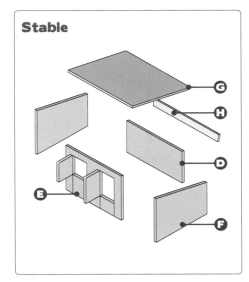

Tractor shed

Item	Qty	Length	Width	Thickness	Diameter	Material
1 Front/Back	2	252	190	6		Ply
2 Beams	7	178	18	8		Red Pine
3 High end	1	190	178	3		Ply
4 Low end	1	136	178	3		Ply
5 Roof	1	304	206	3		Ply
6 Roof edging long	2	304	18	8		Red Pine
7 Roof edging short	2	190	18	8		Red Pine

Pigsty

Item	Qty	Length	Width	Thickness	Diameter	Material
1 Front/Back	2	216	90	8		Ply
2 End	2	132	94	10		Ply
3 Roof beam	1	196	10	10		Red Pine
4 Rear roof	1	240	88	3		Ply
5 Front roof	1	240	84	3		Ply
6 Pen sides	3	72	44	8		Ply
7 Pen front	1	216	44	8		Ply

Farm house

Item	Qty	Length	Width	Thickness	Diameter	Material
A Side	2	334	148	6		Ply
B Beams	6	204	12	12		Red Pine
C Back	1	244	204	3		Ply
D Front	1	234	204	3		Ply
E Grooves	2	204	12	12		Red Pine
F Window ledges	4	48	10	4		Red Pine
G Window ledges	4	44	10	4		Red Pine
H Door ledge	1	54	10	4		Red Pine
I Floors	2	192	148	3		Ply
J Roof	2	246	150	6		Ply
K Chimney	1	370	38	20		Red Pine
L Chimney ledge	1	40	22	3		Ply
M Perspex	1	234	204	2		Perspex

Dutch barn

Item	Qty	Length	Width	Thickness	Diameter	Material
A Sides	2	260	208	6		Ply
B Beams	7	174	18	8		Red Pine
C Roof	1	230	206	3		Ply

Stable

Item	Qty	Length	Width	Thickness	Diameter	Material
D Back	1	196	100	8		Ply
E Front	1	196	140	8		Ply
F End	2	180	140	8		Ply
G Roof	1	210	228	6		Ply
H Roof support	1	228	20	6		Red Pine

Implement shed

This is where the tractor, trailer, Land Rover and so on are kept. The plywood design allows for the shed to be stretched if necessary.

1 Pencil in the bits to be cut out and cut away the waste pieces.

2 Strips of wood are made to fit the slots you've cut out. Glue these in place.

3 The strips are very quickly fitted to the implement shed, but a word of warning if using hot glue as it comes out at boiling point and can burn you, so great care is needed. However, speed is essential to get the best bonding between the pieces.

4 Use a carpenter's square to ensure that the shed wall is upright and that the strip of timber attached is at 90° to the wall. This is exactly how to check it.

5 The back of the shed is now glued on.

6 Check the uprights again.

7 A top spar is now added to start forming the roof.

8 It's surprising just how fast the building grows.

9 The last spar is fitted ready for the walls and roof.

10 The wall is glued in place.

11 The same at the other end.

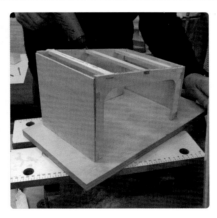

12 Both walls in place.

13 The roof is glued on.

Pigsty

This farm has a traditional pigsty, and again the design can be stretched to accommodate more pig pens.

1 The front of the pigsty is shaped. Make sure that the door is sufficiently large for your pigs!

2 The ends are identical. The cut-down side of the wall is the same thickness as the front wall, and with glue fits snugly together.

3 The front wall and side going together.

4 Using a carpenter's square, check for squareness.

5 The second end is fitted. Check that it's at 90° to the front.

6 Front, back and sides fitted.

7 The sty front wall being fitted.

8 The dividing wall in place.

9 The roof comes next. You have to be quick with the glue gun, otherwise the glue cools and the joint is not so good.

10 The other section of the roof is now fitted and put in place rapidly.

Farmhouse

You can't really have a farm without a farmhouse. I've used the same construction method for the house as for the implement shed.

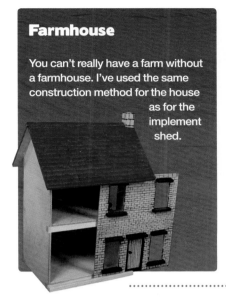

1 Two pieces of ply are taped together, then cuts for the spars/battens are marked in.

2 The cut-outs are made for the battens.

3 The roof pitch is cut to shape.

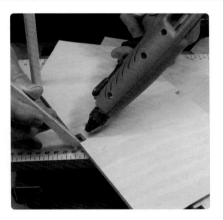

4 The battens are glued into the side of the house wall.

5 The house grows rapidly – don't forget to check it with a square as you go.

6 The ground floor is fitted.

7 The first floor is fitted, and it's looking something like a house.

8 The front of the house is marked out.

9 Bore a hole in the window waste, insert the saw blade and then cut out the windows.

10 The front wall of the house needs to be removable. I decided against hinges – the front wall slides to either side instead. To make a sliding door you need an L-shaped piece of timber. I fitted my Dremel into the shape/router table and adjusted the cutter so that it would cut the desired rebate.

11 Now glue the rebated timber to the front of the house – one piece at the bottom and the other at the top. I've allowed sufficient width in the rebate for a piece of Perspex to be glued to the window and door area.

12 The front wall slides easily in the rebated timber. To prevent 'snagging' I just glued a complete piece of Perspex the size of the front wall.

13 To add a touch of realism, windowsills are formed from pieces of timber and hot-glued in place.

14 This transforms the front of the house and makes it look real – fiddly, but worth the effort.

15 Now for the roof – that takes a lot of glue.

16 The second side is then glued. The roof is pressed down and held for a minute while the glue cures.

17 Now if you really want to alter a bland-looking wall, try this. Dremel make a gas-powered soldering iron. There's a range of tips that fit it, and this one is burning bricks on to the wall – how's that for a bit of realism?

The other farm buildings – the Dutch barn and the horse stable – follow the same method of construction. Fences are made from thin pieces of batten, the rails from barbecue wood skewers. Britains make a wonderful selection of farm animals. There are different sizes, so make sure that the pigs and horses fit their sty and stable!

Ark & animals

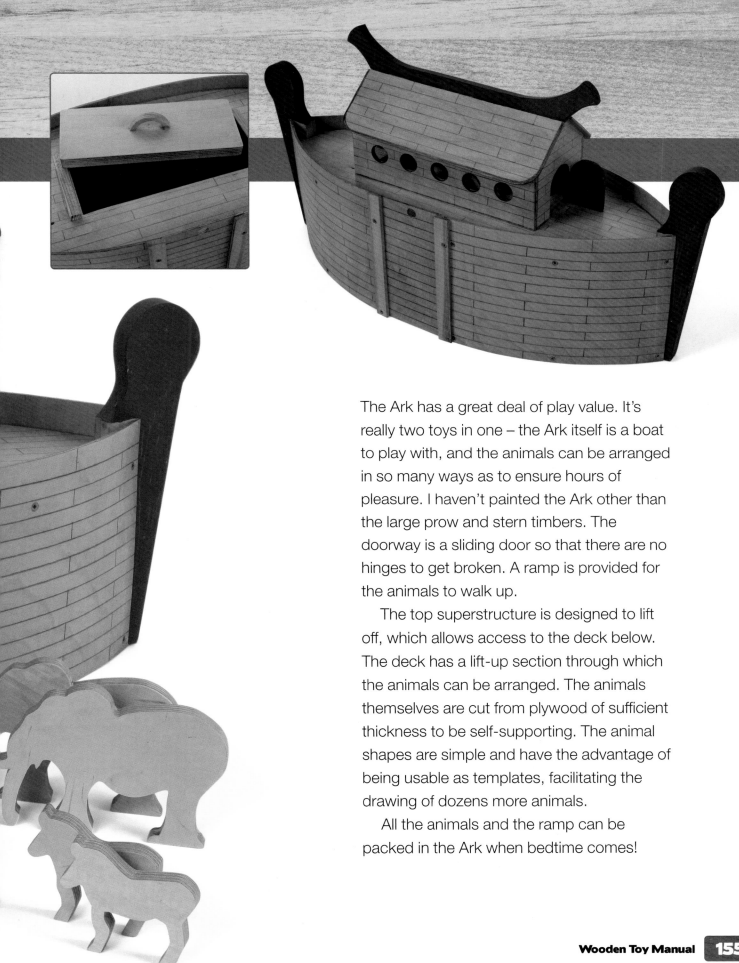

The Ark has a great deal of play value. It's really two toys in one – the Ark itself is a boat to play with, and the animals can be arranged in so many ways as to ensure hours of pleasure. I haven't painted the Ark other than the large prow and stern timbers. The doorway is a sliding door so that there are no hinges to get broken. A ramp is provided for the animals to walk up.

The top superstructure is designed to lift off, which allows access to the deck below. The deck has a lift-up section through which the animals can be arranged. The animals themselves are cut from plywood of sufficient thickness to be self-supporting. The animal shapes are simple and have the advantage of being usable as templates, facilitating the drawing of dozens more animals.

All the animals and the ramp can be packed in the Ark when bedtime comes!

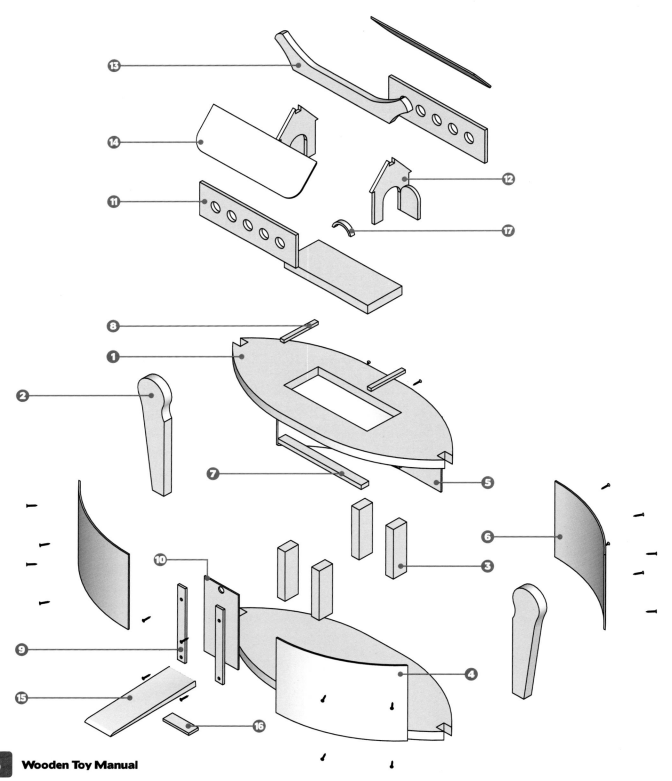

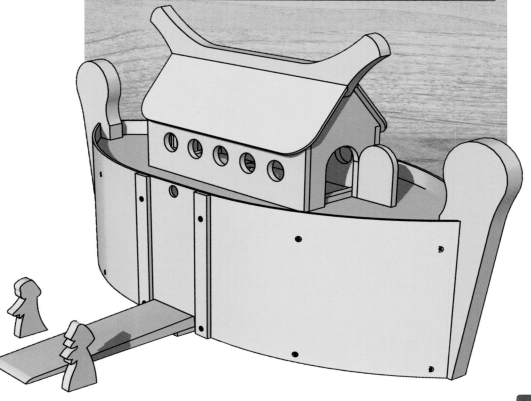

Cutting list

Item	Qty	Length	Width	Thickness	Diameter	Material
1 Base/deck	2	560	230	20		Ply
2 Bow/Stern Supports	2	260	70	20		Red Pine
3 Internal supports	4	35	20	116		Red Pine
4 Port side hull	2	290	176	3		Ply
5 Starboard side hull	1	360	176	3		Ply
6 Starboard side hull	1	280	176	3		Ply
7 Hatch supports	2	220	20	10		Red Pine
8 Cabin supports	2	90	10	7		Red Pine
9 Door supports	2	176	20	5		Red Pine
10 Door	1	176	90	3		Ply
11 Side	2	254	78	7		Ply
12 End	2	130	104	7		Ply
13 Top	1	350	70	14		Red Pine
14 Roof	2	272	90	3		Ply
15 Ramp	1	224	68	14		Red Pine
16 Ramp support	1	68	25	6		Ply
17 Hatch handle	1	50	10	5		Ply

1 Plywood is such a useful modelling timber, as it comes in many sizes and thicknesses. Make a start by marking out two identical 'discs' of plywood.

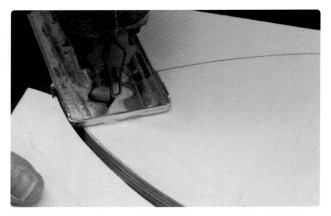

2 Clamp the plywood firmly to the workstation and, using a fine-cutting plywood blade, cut them out.

3 Once cut out, tidy up the edges with glass paper – note the two cut-outs at either end made ready for the prow and stern timbers.

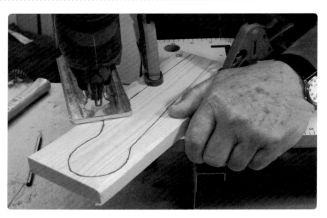

4 Having marked the prow and stern timbers, firmly clamp them to the workstation and cut them out with the jigsaw. A hand is necessary to steady the workstation.

5 The top of the stern timber jigsawed to shape. Now cut the rest out.

6 The Sanding Band gets to work removing any saw cuts and doing the final shaping.

7 The prow and stern timbers are now fixed into the base (have a 'dry run' first without the glue, just to make sure that it all fits).

8 There are four central pillars determining the height of the deck above the base.

9 Now fit the deck. It may be necessary to shave off little pieces of the plywood to get these timbers to fit. Ideally you want a tight fit for these parts.

10 This is the gluing stage. The top deck is fitted and rests on the four central pillars. The stern and prow timbers are glued into place. All this is a fairly busy operation and an extra pair of hands is extremely useful.

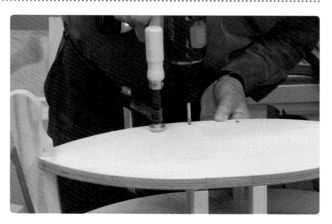

11 Use a large clamp to ensure that the deck is resting on the pillars beneath. Now bore a pilot hole, countersink it, and drive a screw into the pillar beneath.

12 You'll need to do this for all four pillars.

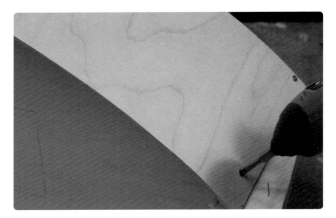

13 A sheet of very thin (3mm) plywood is bent around the curved section to meet the prow. You'll need to bend this a few times and perhaps trim it to size before screwing it to the deck. Final trimming should be left until the fixing is done.

14 Forming the doorway by screwing strips of timber to the plywood skins. Note that the timber being screwed has an overlap.

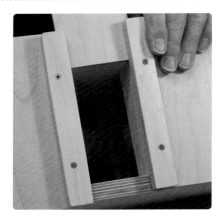

15 Screw the timber to the pillar below. The overlap allows for a sliding door to be fitted.

16 Now repeat on the other side, making sure to create an overlap.

17 Now the sliding door can be fitted. If it's a bit tight skim a little off the sides and use a sander on the door – this will ease everything up.

18 Bore a small hole in the top of the door, just big enough for a child's finger to pull the door up and down. The plywood on the other side has no door. Screw a sheet of plywood on.

19 Now the superstructure has to be made. The deck-house is being cut out. The two ends are so shaped that the sides fit into them rather than on to the ends.

20 The roof spar is shaped. It gives an interesting shape to the deck-house.

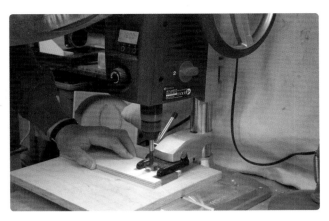

21 The sides have circular windows – it's so much easier to drill a round window than a square hole. I think the round holes look much better too. Both sides were taped together and the windows were cut in both simultaneously.

22 The ends of the deck-house have doors that are glued to the sides.

23 I used the hot glue gun for this task, as it's excellent for rapidly fixing small pieces.

24 Glue is applied to the ends of the deck-house.

25 Side fitted to the end. Check that it's square.

26 The assembled deck-house now has the decorative roof ridge timber fitted. This fits into the pre-cut slots in both ends.

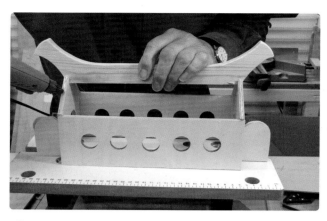

27 Glue is being applied to the ends to fix the roof.

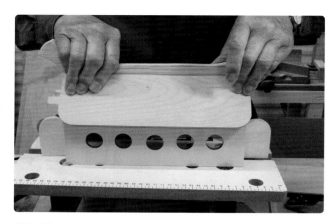

28 The roof is pressed and held in place for a minute for the glue to cure and hold it.

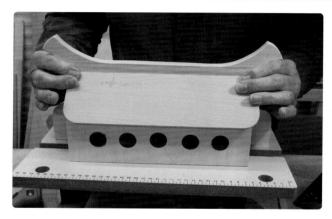

29 The second roof panel is fitted.

30 Now is the time to remove the square look of the decorative roof ridge board. Work off the edges to create a really smooth ridge board – it looks so much more effective.

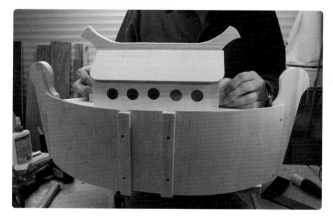

31 Just about ready for the flood – but wait, we need some animals!

32 I started with a giraffe from a waste piece of ply. It's best to use the largest offcuts first, and the smaller pieces for the smaller animals.

33 Well, the giraffes are on board, and now we just need the rest – oh, and don't forget it's two of each!

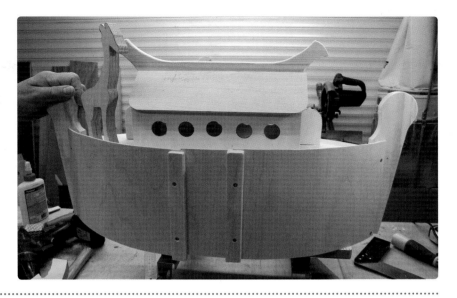

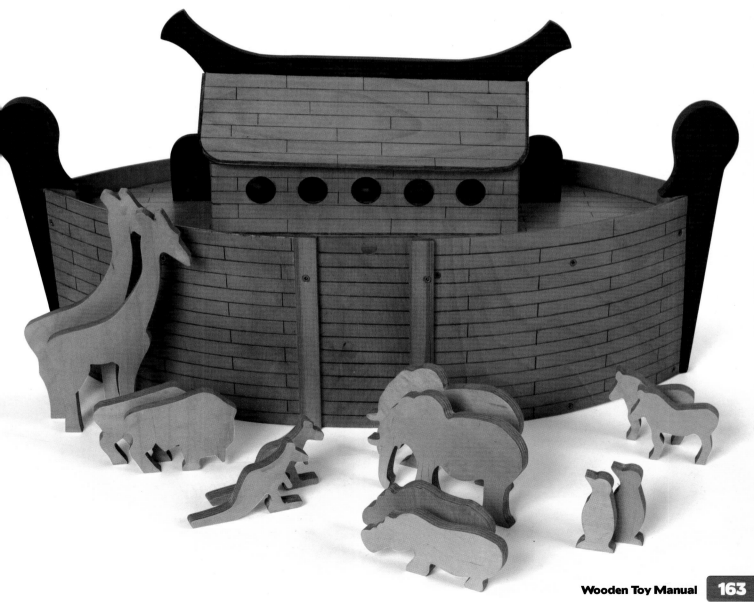

Crane

When I was a boy Tri-ang made a wonderful red crane. The boom was adjustable and it had wheels. Positioned at the top of the stairwell, one could wind objects right to the ground floor and spend hours doing it. The winding handle had a ratchet, so the operation could be halted at any time for offloading on the landing below. I've since seen one on BBC's *The Antiques Road Show*.

I've tried to replicate this crane here, adding some extras – e.g. working jack feet. I hope that some child somewhere will have as much pleasure operating this crane as I did my Tri-ang version some 50-plus years ago.

Crane

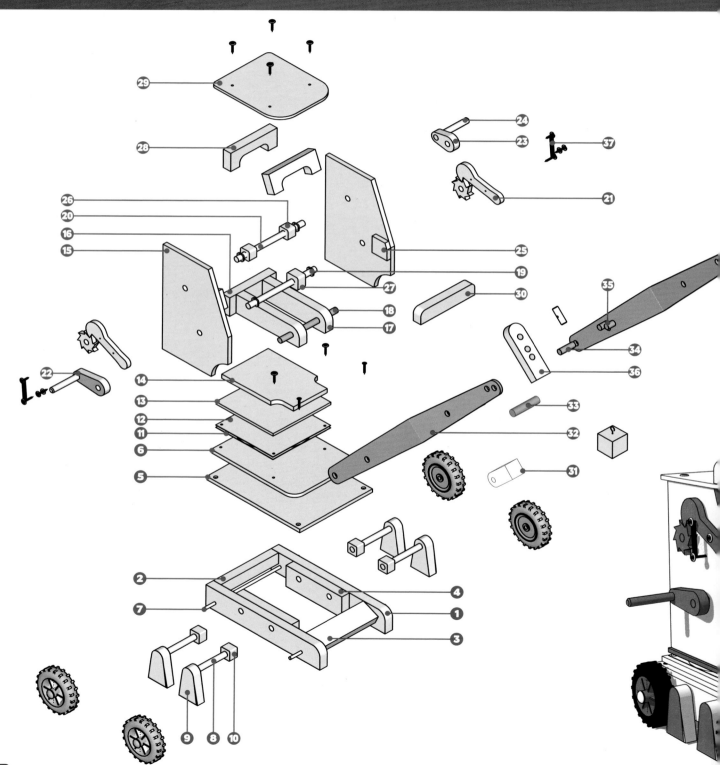

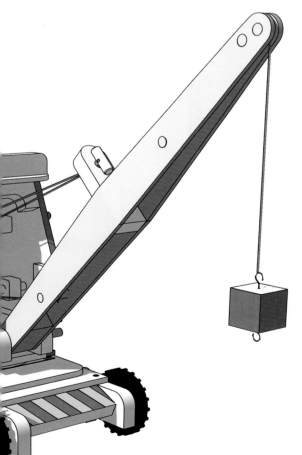

Cutting list

Item		Qty	Length	Width	Thickness	Diameter	Material
1	Sides	2	306	50	20		Red Pine
2	Rear support	1	154	26	20		Red Pine
3	Front support	1	154	44	20		Red Pine
4	Side supports	2	150	50	20		Red Pine
5	Top	1	250	194	8		Ply
6	Top plate	1	224	172	8		Ply
7	Axels	2	254			6	Steel
8	Hydraulic jack rods	4	110			12	Dowel
9	Hydraulic jacks	4	76	50	20		Red Pine
10	Hydraulic jack ends	4	24	24	20		Red Pine
11	Metal Plates	2	154	154	1		
12	Bearings	1				154	
13	Base	1	154	164	6		Ply
14	Base plate	1	176	124	10		Ply
15	Sides	2	252	176	10		Ply
16	Back support	1	124	44	20		Red Pine
17	Arm support	2	170	44	20		Red Pine
18	Arm axel	1	150			12	Dowel
19	Arm winch axel	1	178			12	Dowel
20	Load winch axel	1	178			12	Dowel
21	Arm/Load winch release lever	2	120	46	10		Ply
22	Load winch handle arm	1	84	35	15		Ply
23	Arm winch handle arm	1	60	35	15		Ply
24	Winch handle	2	85			12	Dowel
25	Arm/Load winch handle supports	2	40	40	10		Ply
26	Winch axel blocks	2	24	24	20		Red Pine
27	Load axel block	1	30	30	20		Red Pine
28	Roof support	2	124	44	20		Red Pine
29	Roof	1	184	154	6		Ply
30	Roof top support		144	30	20		Red Pine
31	Pivot block	1	80	37	35		Red Pine
32	Arm sides	2	612	54	6		Ply
33	Arm bottom dowel support	1	50			12	Dowel
34	Arm mid dowel support	1	37			12	Dowel
35	Arm top dowel support	2	37			12	Dowel
36	Arm separator	1					Red Pine
37	Spring						

1 As always, start with the chassis and tape the timbers together. Measure and mark for the axle holes. Also mark in the curved section of the chassis.

2 Drill the axle holes.

3 Fix the chassis in the vice and, using the band sander, shape the ends,

4 Still with both chassis members taped together bore the holes for the jacks.

5 Tapes removed and axles in place, clearly showing the holes bored to take the dowel rods that will hold the jacks.

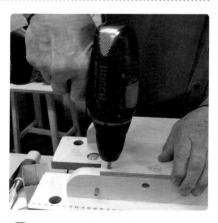

6 Now screw the platform on to the chassis.

7 Carefully mark out the crane body.

8 The crane body sides must be taped together. The holes bored for the winding-rods will then line up.

9 With the two sides still taped together, do the shaping.

10 A batten is glued and screwed on to the floor of the winding house. This is fixed at the back.

11 Now glue is applied to the edges of the floor.

12 The sides of the winding house are now positioned – I used a clamp to hold things together, and pushed the winding-rods through the prepared holes.

13 Shaped blocks are glued into the winding house.

14 A second clamp is used to hold things together.

15 And another clamp. It's very important to keep checking that things are square, and that the winding handle dowel rods turn freely.

16 Now, back to the chassis while the glue dries on the winding house. Shaped blocks of wood form the hydraulic jack legs (which all cranes have when they start lifting). Bore holes in the blocks to take the dowel rods.

17 With hole bored, the jacks need cutting to shape. Cut all four jacks to shape.

18 The jacks need to slide easily out of the chassis. It may be necessary to slightly enlarge the holes in the chassis.

19 Further blocks are fitted on the inside edges of the chassis to give the jacks a good bearing surface to slide on.

20 Now fit a dowel rod and see how well it slides in and out. Do the same for all four jacks.

21 The jacks are fitted to the dowel rods.

22 The chassis upside down to show what things should look like. A little glue carefully placed between the blocks will hold things together. Be careful not to get any glue on the dowel rods.

23 The chassis right side up with the jacks extended.

24 At the base of the jib is a substantial block of wood that holds it together. This block is actually a pivot block as well, with the dowel rod going through it.

25 The jib arms are taped together and holes bored.

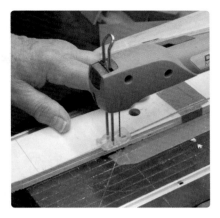

26 The arms are cut to shape.

27 Now start to assemble the jib. Glue is applied to the dowel rods and pushed into place.

28 The pivot block is glued on to the arms.

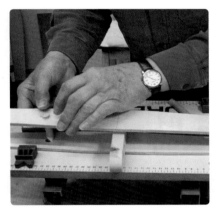

29 Assemble the rest of the dowel rods – you can't avoid getting your fingers sticky!

30 Squeeze the arms on to the dowel rods.

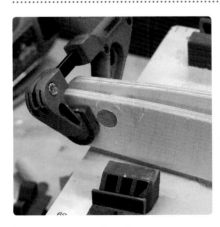

31 Once the dowel rods are in place it's necessary to use clamps until the glue cures.

32 The jib now needs to be fitted into the winding house.

33 Two lengths of timber are fitted into the winding house.

34 The timbers that go either side of the jib are now screwed into the winding house. Screws are driven through the bottom to hold the timbers.

35 Next a ratchet is cut in plywood.

36 The ratchet is glued on to the dowel rod, and at the other side of the winding house a cranking handle is made and glued to the dowel rod.

39 Glue is applied to the winding mechanism that operates the boom. The ratchet/pawl for this is on the other side. The boom is anchored to the centre spacer. A dowel rod is drilled and used as a toggle. As the handle for the boom is rotated the toggle tightens on the centre spacer and the boom is raised and lowered. The winding handle is fitted.

37 Now cut the brake/pawl that fits the ratchet. The lower ratchet and winding handle actuate the crane's lifting hook.

38 The brake/pawl is secured to the side by screws. A cup washer fits between the brake and the side and another one beneath the screw head.

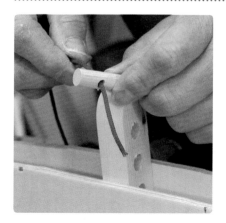

42 The twin cords can be tied off around the dowel rod. Alternatively, if heavy loads are envisaged the block shown on the dowel rod is fitted with a screw eye, on to which the winding cord is tied.

40 The boom is anchored to the centre spacer. A dowel rod is drilled and used as a toggle.

41 As the handle is turned the toggle is pulled up tight on to the spacer and the boom can be raised or lowered.

43 The boom is rigged and the block and tackle line is fitted. I used a large cup hook and square blocks of wood as the lifting block.

44 Next the winding house and chassis have to be fixed together. I used a large turntable or ball race. These are used to turn televisions and small bookcases and are available in a whole range of sizes. It will depend on exactly where the attachment/screw holes are placed in the ball race as to how you do this.

45 I cut a separate sheet of ply to fit on the chassis top. Screw the ball race to it. Now turn the winding house upside down and rotate the ball race until the fixing holes are found. Screw the winding house to the ball race. Turn the winding house the right way up and screw the separate sheet of ply to the chassis. This is much easier than it sounds – honestly!

46 Screw the roof on but don't glue it. In the future you may wish to replace worn cables. The crane should end up looking something like this. It's well worth the struggle.

Articulated lorry

The lorry and the crane make a good working unit and both provide lots of play value for youngsters. I haven't built a very complex cab, but it does form the basis for you to add lots more detail.

Articulated lorry

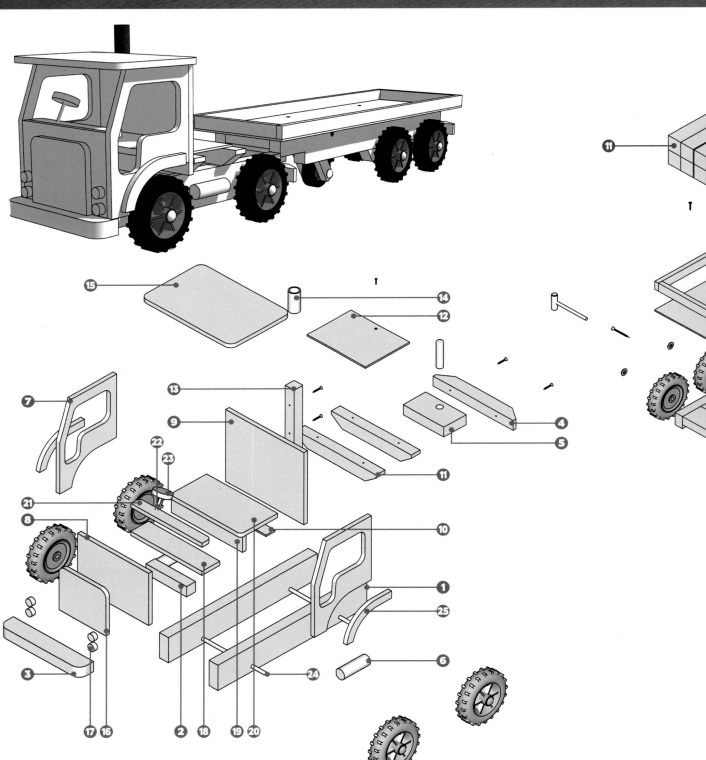

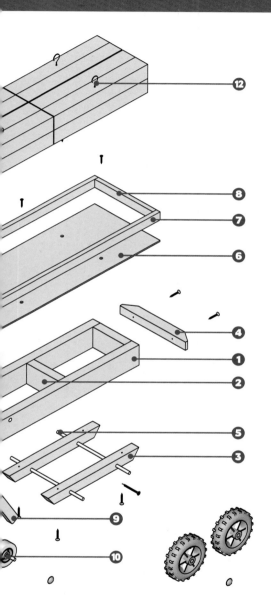

Cab

Item		Qty	Length	Width	Thickness	Diameter	Material
1	Chasis side	2	330	50	20		Red Pine
2	Front support	1	90	20	20		Red Pine
3	Front bumper	1	178	32	20		Red Pine
4	Rear bumper	1	178	24	20		Red Pine
5	Hitch mounting	1	90	50	20		Red Pine
6	Fuel tanks	2	58			20	Dowel
7	Cab side	2	176	126	8		Ply
8	Cab front	1	158	102	8		Ply
9	Cab back	1	174	143	8		Ply
10	Cab back support	1	130	20	3		Ply
11	Trailer mounts	2	178	24	20		Red Pine
12	Trailer platform	1	130	98	3		Ply
13	Exhaust pipe	1	125	20	20		Red Pine
14	Exhaust pipe top	1	40			20	hose
15	Roof	1	200	134	8		Red Pine
16	Radiator	1	104	86	8		Ply
17	Lights	4			8	14	Ply
18	Cab floor	1	158	40	8		Ply
19	Seat support	1	158	30	8		Ply
20	Seat	1	158	82	8		Ply
21	Dash	1	158	20	8		Ply
22	Steering column	1	35			4	Dowel
23	Steering wheel	1			8	34	Ply
24	Axels	2	196			6	Steel
25	Mudguards	2	98	58			Ply

Trailer

Item		Qty	Length	Width	Thickness	Diameter	Material
1	Chasis sides	2	480	50	20		Red Pine
2	Chasis supports	3	86	50	20		Red Pine
3	Axel supports	2	246	22	20		Red Pine
4	Rear bumper	1	178	24	20		Red Pine
5	Rear axels	2	196			6	Steel
6	Load bed	1	540	178	3		Ply
7	Load sides	2	540	20	10		Red Pine
8	Load ends	2	158	20	10		Red Pine
9	Wheel support	1	120	50	20		Red Pine
10	Front axel	1	60			6	Steel
11	Blocks (load)	16	254	34	34		Red pine
12	Hooks	4					

1 Mark out the front bumper that forms an integral part of the chassis.

2 Now cut to shape the recesses that take the two longitudinal chassis members.

3 Rounding off the corners with the circular band sander.

4 The two longitudinal chassis members are taped together, the axle hole is pencilled in and then they're drilled as a pair.

5 Slip the axles in place. I tend to drill axle holes very slightly larger than the axles.

6 Glue the front bumper on.

7 It's important to clamp the wood while the glue cures.

8 The tow hitch and rear bumper are fitted at the back of the chassis.

9 Glue, clamp and screw the rear bumper on. The trailer hitch fits between the chassis.

10 The cab is then shaped up. Plywood is the ideal timber for this job.

11 Once the cab sides have been cut out, run the band-sander around the edges to tidy up.

12 You'll need clamps and patience to fit the cab together. Don't apply the glue until you have a good fit.

13 It's probably easiest to glue the sides to the back for starters and then slide the front of the cab in place and put a clamp on it.

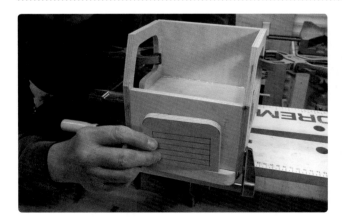

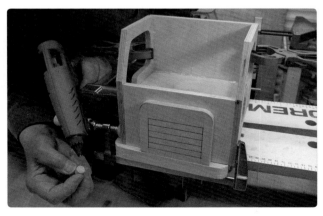

14 I pencilled-in the radiator grill, but you can make more of this feature, maybe by actually routing out the radiator grooves.

15 I used wood plugs for the headlamps and hot glue to fix them in place.

16 Fit the seat and glue the roof on.

17 If you intend to add more cab detail then don't fix the roof at this point.

18 Screw the bearers on to the chassis.

19 Glue the cab into position.

20 Glue the exhaust stack on to the back of the cab. The protruding dowel rod has a piece of rubber tube on the end to prevent accidents.

21 The tow hitch is glued into position.

22 A large diameter dowel rod doubles up as a fuel tank. To ensure it sticks to the chassis I planed it flat on the back – this provides a far greater glue area.

23 The tractor unit should look something like this.

24 Both trailer chassis timbers are taped together, fixed in the jaws of the workstation, and the cut-out is made. This cut-out section fits over the back of the lorry chassis.

25 A tenon saw makes this an easy cut.

26 Two identical pieces of timber are now drilled together as a pair. The trailer axles are threaded into the holes and the timbers screwed on to the chassis members.

27 Next the tow hitch block is glued into the chassis.

28 The shaped block of wood is now glued into the end of the chassis.

29 The rear bumper is screwed on to the end of the chassis.

30 The trailer deck is now prepared. Using a black lead pencil, mark in the plank lines...

31 ...then draw lines across these to represent the ends of the planks.

32 Now screw the deck to the chassis.

33 Make sure that you position the screws carefully so that they go into the chassis members.

34 Small strips of timber are glued on to the trailer deck.

35 The edging prevents the blocks of wood falling off.

36 Holes are bored in the chassis to make the pivot point for the jockey wheel.

37 A small section is cut from the centre of a length of timber, in which a small wheel is held in place by an axle rod.

38 Screws are driven in from both sides of the chassis to hold the assembly between the chassis frames. I also inserted two sections of plastic pipe to keep the jockey wheel assembly central. The screws go through the plastic pipe and effectively act as washers.

39 The trailer with wheels in place and jockey wheel down.

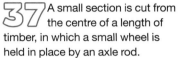

Bagatelle

My mother had a bagatelle board, and I can remember spending hours shooting balls around the board and getting very excited when I hit a high score. Having discovered that catapult shot (available from gun shops) is the ideal size ball for this game, I designed the board and bolt-firing mechanism around this. Earlier I'd experimented with large ball bearings, but these proved too heavy for the spring bolt mechanism to fire to the top of the board.

Bagatelle

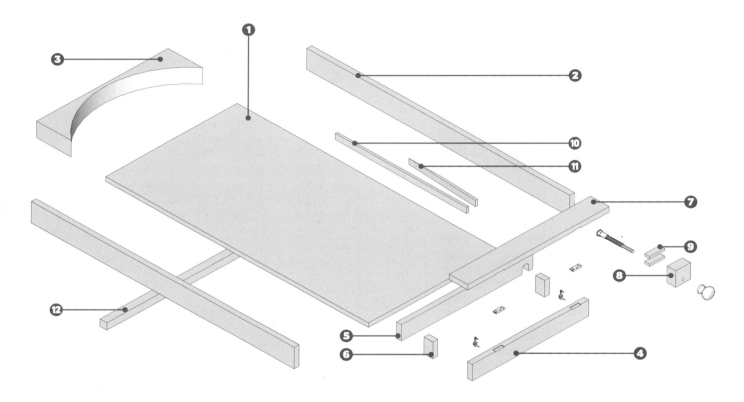

Cutting list

Item	Qty	Length	Width	Thickness	Diameter	Material
1 Base	1	760	378	12		Ply
2 Side	2	760	55	14		Red Pine
3 Curved end block	1	378	100	43		Red Pine
4 Box front	1	335	43	14		Red Pine
5 Box back	1	378	43	14		Red Pine
6 Box side	2	43	26	12		Ply
7 Box lid	1	406	54	14		Red Pine
8 Firing bolt block	1	43	43	25		Red Pine
9 Firing bolt block supports	2	43	15	6		Red Pine
10 Long rail	1	380	16	6		Red Pine
11 Short rail	1	210	16	6		Red Pine
12 Table leg	1	406	20	20		Red Pine

1 Select a good quality plywood board. My personal preference is Nordic birch plywood – it's more expensive, but the ply is of excellent quality. Prepare the board by giving it a light sanding with fine grade paper.

2 The most difficult job in the project is to cut the curved section at the top of the board. This needs to be done carefully, otherwise an irregular surface will deflect the ball. I marked the curve out with a piece of string and a pencil.

Fix the timber very carefully in the workstation, and then, most importantly, select the right blade for the jigsaw. I used Bosch T234X, called the 'Progressor'. It's a stonkingly big blade, but cuts well and fairly evenly, and this is a large chunk of wood and does need a big blade. As you cut the curve, feed the jigsaw steadily into the wood, and resist any temptation to push the machine sideways if you cut off the line. Try always to push the machine steadily forwards. As the cut progresses you'll have to reposition the wood as you cut the curve.

3 Once the curve is cut out it should hopefully look something like this. Don't be disturbed if there are a few irregularities, as these can be removed with a large diameter dowel rod and garnet stone paper or similar.

4 Work the inside of the curve until all the sawing marks are removed. Be careful at the edges, as this is end grain and will break off.

5 I used the band sander on the edges as it's important that there's no 'lip' where the side will join the corner.

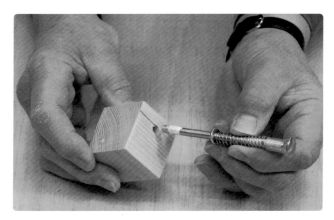

6 Making the spring ball-firing mechanism proved far less complicated than I'd expected. A hole was bored in the block of wood and a coach bolt was selected that was of sufficient length and diameter. This bolt needs to be a loose fit in the block of wood.

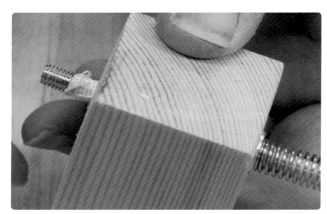

7 Thread the bolt through the wood and wind a length of PTFE tape along the threaded section of the bolt. This tape is used by plumbers when making a joint – it's thin and winds into threads.

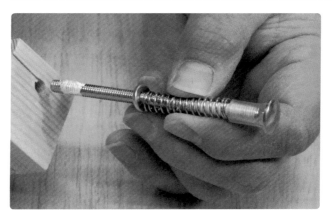

8 The bolt has a couple of springs (bought from Machine Mart), and a washer behind them. The washer is vital to the works, as it prevents the spring going into the bolt hole.

9 A standard wooden knob is screwed on to the end of the bolt. Drill a small pilot hole in the bolt and gently thread the knob on to the bolt. The PTFE tape helps to pack the thread and keep the knob in place.

10 Preparing to glue the whole board together. Glue is applied to the top curved section.

11 The top is secured to the board using clamps. Now, glue is slippery when it's clamped, so you must check that the clamping action doesn't make the piece slide out of position.

12 Glue is now applied to both sides.

13 The bolt-firing mechanism is glued into position.

14 Note the cut-out on this timber, allowing it to fit over the bolt. Check it fits.

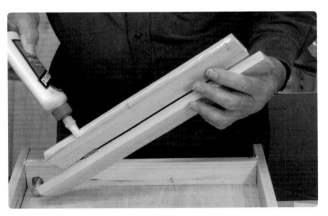

15 Apply the glue and fit the timber in place.

16 I hinged a flap into the back panel. This flap forms the lid, which makes a storage cupboard for the balls. Note the cut-out section at the bottom that fits against the ball-firing mechanism.

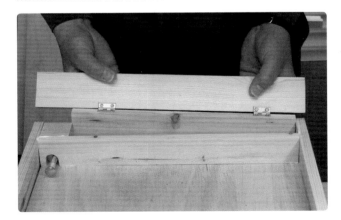

17 Fit the back section.

18 A sash clamp is fitted to hold the sides and back panels while the glue dries. A sash clamp is also fitted at the top. Check that the clamping pressure hasn't altered where the pieces should be.

19 When the balls are fired they need to always go to the top of the board. To guide the balls to the top a strip of timber is glued to the board.

20 The strip of timber is fitted.

21 Use a compass to mark in the various 'cages' that will catch the balls. You can make these as easy or as difficult as you like.

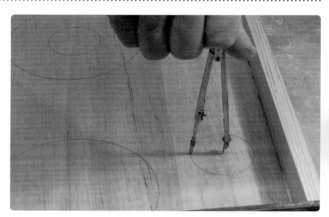

22 A very small cage with a high score.

If you can find them, brass escutcheon pins are ideal. They have a good head and give the board a really professional look. These pins can be hard to find on the High Street unless you have a really good old-fashioned ironmonger, but they're relatively easy to trace online.

23 Driving the pins in is tricky. The simplest method is to make a small hole with a bradawl...

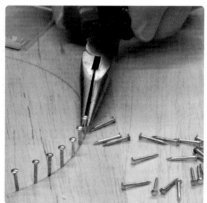

24 ...hold the pin with a pair of long-nosed pliers...

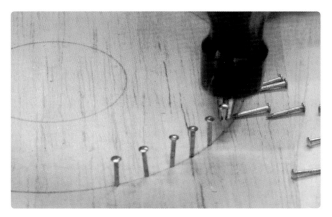

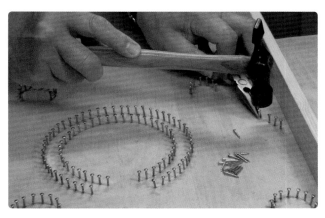

25 ...and tap the pin in with a small hammer. This method certainly prevents the 'ouch' factor in this job.

26 I found that a row of pins placed in strategic places in the 'ball run' makes for some interesting scores

NB: I found that it's best to create a board that's not too crowded with cages, otherwise when you fire the balls you'll find they all follow the same track. Place one or two pins in their path. The balls will then deflect and end up spreading themselves in different directions. From then on it's the use of the firing mechanism that determines the score. Good luck!

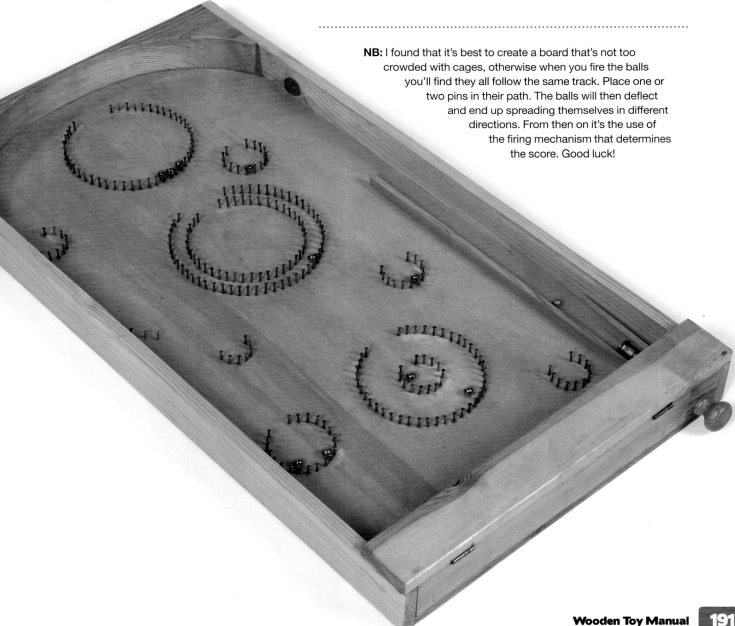

Labyrinth

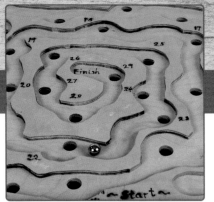

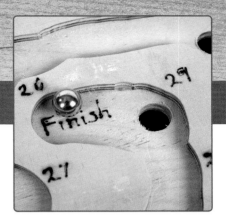

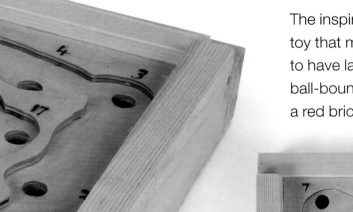

The inspiration to make this game came from a wooden toy that my grandfather had. Ball-rolling games appear to have lasting appeal, and I can certainly remember a ball-bouncing computer game designed to knock down a red brick wall in the early years of computer games.

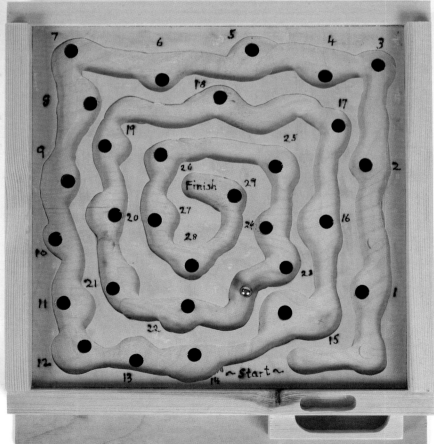

Labyrinth

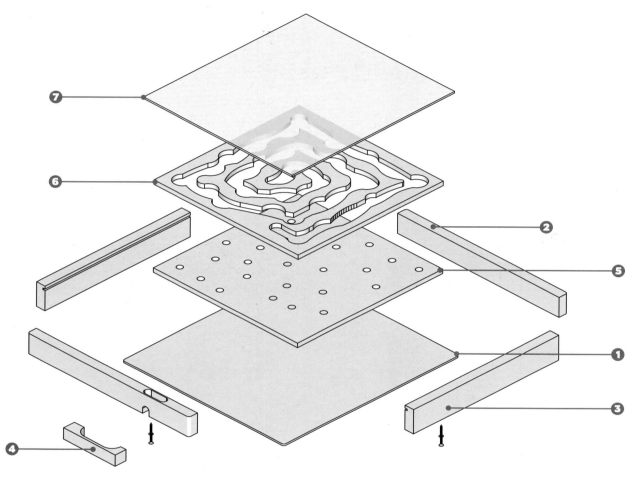

Cutting list

Item	Qty	Length	Width	Thickness	Diameter	Material
1 Base	1	324	300	3		Ply
2 Front/back edge	2	300	36	16		Red Pine
3 Sides	2	268	44	16		Red Pine
4 Ball holder	1	96	20	20		Red Pine
5 Top with holes	1	268	268	8		Ply
6 Maze top	1	268	268	8		Ply
7 Perspex	1	300	276	3		Perspex

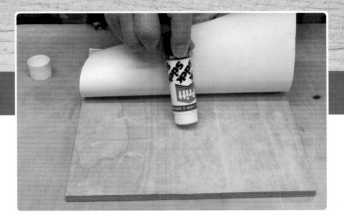

1 I started by drawing a labyrinth on to a piece of paper. I sketched in the trackway and the positions of the holes. It's simple to make it just too difficult, so be kind to yourself and have a generous track width.

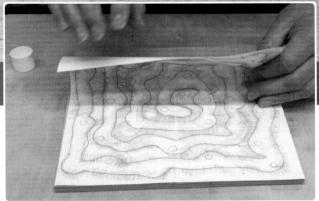

2 The piece of paper is then glued on to a sheet of plywood, the idea being that you can use a router to cut out the track and, guided by this paper 'map', make no mistakes.

3 A small router such as the Dremel Trio is ideal for such a cutting operation. You need a router bit with a 'bottom cut' to create the ideal track.

4 It's important to be able to see the map as you cut, so if dust extraction is available then it's a good idea to use it.

5 Routing out is a fairly dusty job. I used a small paintbrush to dust the track and make sure that I was on target.

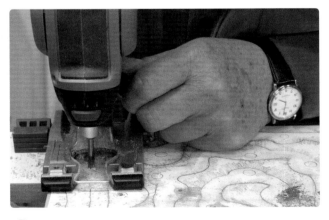

6 You can see here that the operator has good visibility as the job progresses. An adjustable handle makes it easier to deal with all the curves.

7 Once the track is cut out, mark the positions for the holes and then cut them out.

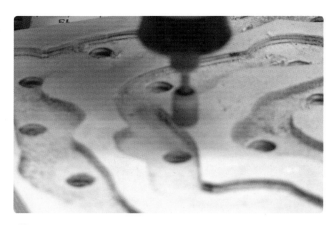

8 With the band sander, work along the sides of the track smoothing everything over.

9 The labyrinth is covered with a sheet of Perspex. Buy the Perspex before you decide on the groove that has to be cut in the side timbers.

10 Fit a router cutter the same thickness as the Perspex, or marginally larger. Clamp the timber to the workstation and route out the groove. The lightweight and powerful Trio is perfect for this job.

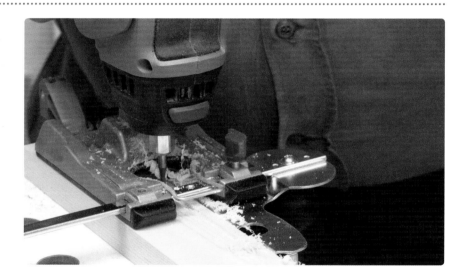

11 The labyrinth has four surrounds. Two of the side pieces have a groove for the Perspex. The other two are lower to allow the Perspex to slide over them.

12 Make sure that the ends are positioned in such a way that the Perspex can be slid in and out. Now glue up. Sash clamps are used to glue the sides around the labyrinth.

13 The base is plywood and is only screwed in place (in case a ball gets jammed in the works).

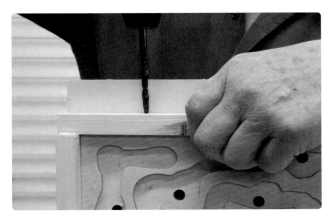

14 A large hole is bored at the back beneath the 'deck' and can be enlarged with the band sander.

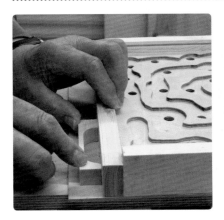

15 I cut out a small slotted timber to act as a ball catcher. This is glued on to the lip of the base but not to the side.

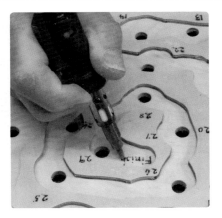

16 I then used the Dremel VersaTip soldering iron to burn 'Start', 'Finish' and the numbers of each hole into the plywood.

17 Rout a slot in the frame at the back and enlarge it with the band sander if necessary to make the spare ball keeper.

NB: A starting point for the labyrinth is the size of the steel balls you use. Initially I tried ball bearings, but they're very expensive. I then discovered that gun shops keep steel balls for catapults, which I found ideal for the labyrinth and the bagatelle game.

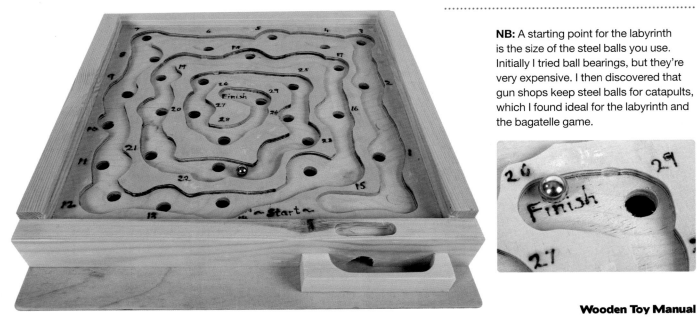

Useful information

The Scandinavian countries supply us with boatloads of red and white pine. Red pine is ideal for so many projects in this book. White pine is ideal for the framework of the playhouse. Their plywoods are also second to none. I've used Scandinavian birch-faced plys extensively in many projects. Scandinavian countries also plant more trees, and consequently grow more timber, than they cut. Newly planted forests are excellent for the environment, and this massive industry is carefully policed and cared for.

Hobby's

A *Hobby's Annual* is published every year. It's an excellent reference source and covers a very wide range of hobbies. This particular catalogue can supply all the wheels I've used in this book, plus the axle rods and the spring caps (of all sizes) to keep the wheels on. An essential read. It's available from good bookshops or direct from Hobby's website at http://hobby.uk.com.

Humbrol

These little tubs of paint are absolutely wonderful for quality and colour range – ideal for any toy-painting job. They're widely available, either from model and hobby shops or from Humbrol's own website at http://www.humbrol.com (tel 01483 233525).

Tools

If you're looking for a general catalogue on tools then probably the one produced by Toolstation of Express Park, Bridgwater, TA6 4RH, will give you the best overview of what's available. Their website can be found at http://www.toolstation.com (email info@toolstation.com, tel 01278 421200).

The specialist catalogue of all the hundreds of tools and accessories produced by Dremel makes a great read. It can be obtained either by writing to Dremel UK, PO Box 98, Broadwater Park, North Orbital Road, Denham, Uxbridge, Middlesex, UB9 5HJ, or by visiting their website at http://www.dremeleurope.com/gb/en/start/index.html (tel 0844 7360109).

If you want a catalogue of the latest DIY power tools available from Bosch, write to Robert Bosch Ltd, Power Tool Division, Broadwater Park, Denham, Uxbridge, UB9 5HJ, or visit http://www.bosch.co.uk (email www.boschpowertools.co.uk, tel 0844 7360 109).

Author's acknowledgements

Many people combine to help an author with a book, not least the members of his family and church. I have to name just a few 'extra specials' who were there at the concept of the idea – and stayed with me to the end:

Mark Hughes – editorial director for Haynes – who must have the patience of the proverbial Job (or should that read 'saint'?), waiting for the text and pictures to arrive.

Paul Gemmell – business development manager for Dremel – who was absolutely tireless in advice, suggestions and practical help. Nothing was too much trouble – I am indebted to you.

Eric Streuli – training manager, power tool division, Robert Bosch – thank you for your humour throughout, and technical advice that's absolutely second to none.

Jonathan Ball – another indispensible member of the team, who has produced some wonderful drawings – in fact, sometimes the drawings look better than the real projects!

Robert Coleman – thank you for many tireless days spent peering through the viewfinder and taking many hundreds of photographs of the projects as they were made.

Derek Smith – a man of genius, who has pulled all the pictures, drawings, cutting lists and text together to make a lovely book. Derek, we salute you.

Katherin Greuel – brand manager, Robert Bosch – who rubber-stamped our requests.

Mark Minton – yard foreman of Bradfords – who always let me search his racks for knot-free timber, and then helped me load the trailer.

Patricia, my wife, who gallantly deciphered my 'sandscript' handwriting and never grumbled about it. I think that she needs a medal!